To:

From:

Date:

TRUE HEART GIRLS
DEVOTIONAL
God's Promises for Me!

for Girls
ages 8-12

Sherry Kyle

Published in association with Books & Such Literary Management, 52 Mission Circle #122, PMB 170, Santa Rosa, CA 95409, www.booksandsuch.com.

ISBN: 978-1-62862-770-1
RoseKidz® reorder# L50019
Juvenile Nonfiction/Religion/Devotion & Prayer

Printed in the United States of America   [1] 5.2018.VP

Table of Contents

Table of Contents

Introduction

Hey!

What would you do if you discovered treasure?

- Would you keep it to yourself?

- Share it with others?

- Or would you bury it so that no one else would find it?

Here is what God's Word says, "I rejoice in your word like one who finds a great treasure." Psalm 119:162, NLT.

Your Bible is a treasure waiting to be read. God's promises are like jewels. God wants you to discover them and not bury them so that you can grow and be confident in who you are and, in turn, share them with others.

In True Heart Girls Devotional: *God's Promises for Me!* there are inspirational messages, stories and questions to make you think. There is a section to write your feelings along with some fun activities. As a tween girl you might feel sad, happy, lonely, or angry, but there are promises in the Bible that you can memorize that will make a difference in your life.

So, let's dig into this book and discover God's treasure—the wonderful promises he has for you!

Secret Message

To decode the secret message, you need to fill out all the missing words after reading the Bible stories. Find the numbered boxes and fill in below. The first letter has been given to you.

T _ _ _ _ _ _ _ _ _ _
  1   2   3   4   5   6   7   8   9   10

_ _ _ _ _ _ _ _
11 12 13 14 15 16 17 18

_ _ _ _ _ _ _ _ _ _ !
19 20 21 22   23 24 25 26 27 28

★ WEEK-1

Day-1

God Forms Families

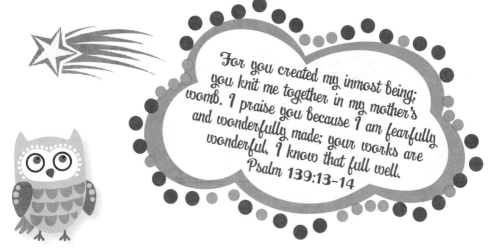

> For you created my inmost being; you knit me together in my mother's womb. I praise you because I am fearfully and wonderfully made; your works are wonderful, I know that full well.
> Psalm 139:13-14

Can I Have Your Family?

Lauren climbed into the bus at 7:30 a.m. She wanted to sleep in, but it was a school day. She found her friend Emma and plopped down next to her.

"Hey, what's wrong with you?" Emma asked.

"You're so lucky." Lauren slumped down in her seat. "Your parents let you go to bed whenever you want, watch TV in your room, and eat dessert every night. My parents are so strict, sometimes I think I was born into the wrong family."

"What happened?" Emma's brows furrowed. "I've never heard you say anything like this before."

"Well, sometimes I wish my parents would bend the rules just a little." Lauren crossed her arms.

"**Whenever** I come to your house, I always have a great time," Emma said. "I wish my parents would spend more time with me like your parents do. I like to stay up late, but just once I wish they'd tell me to go to bed. The way I see it, you have it pretty good."

"Really?" Lauren sat up a litter taller. "I still think having a TV in my room would be cool."

"Well, you are right about that!" Emma laughed. "But I can only turn it on once my homework is done."

Lauren unfolded her arms. "And what about every night?"

Emma bit her lip. "To tell you the truth, I made that part up."

"And to think I was jealous." Lauren giggled. "Maybe I do have great parents."

Emma nodded. "Now you're talking!"

The bus stopped in front of school just in time.

Your Turn

1. Do you ever wish you had your friend's parents? When?

2. Why do you think God chose your family just for you?

11

Bible Story

The Birth of Jesus
Read Luke 2:1-7

Find the Missing Word

Mary was expecting a ⬭ ⬭ ___ ___.

24   15

Write About It

Name your family members who live with you. Remember your pets.

Name your family members who don't live with you.

Tiny Treasure

God always wants the best for you.

Prayer

Lord God, thank you for my family.
I know you chose them just for me.
In Jesus' name, amen.

Do It!

Just as God placed Jesus in the arms of Mary and Joseph, God placed you in YOUR family! Take time to celebrate the family God gave you!

Family Night!

Pita pizza, popcorn and a good family movie will bring everyone together. Have fun!

Pita Pizza

As a family, fill up your pitas with plenty of pizza toppings and enjoy this great meal.

What You Need

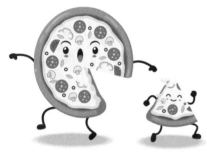

- 1 whole-wheat pita per person
- 1 tablespoon pizza or tomato sauce per pita
- ¼ cup grated mozzarella per pita
- Pepperoni, ham, pineapple, sausage, veggies, or other toppings

What You Do

1. Preheat the oven to 350°F.

2. Split the pita bread halfway around the edge and spoon in the cheese, tomato sauce, and any toppings.

3. Wrap the pita in aluminum foil and bake for 7 to 10 minutes or until the cheese melts.

4. For great movie ideas, search online for "Christian family movies."

God Loves You

> LORD, you are the God of heaven.
> You are a great and wonderful God.
> You keep the covenant you made with those
> who love you and obey your commandments.
> Nehemiah 1:5

I Still Love You

Emily slammed the door shut. She was mad at her stepmom again! Why was Sandy so busy all the time? All Emily wanted was some help with her homework. "What's so bad about that?" she mumbled to herself.

Okay, she knew she took "forever," as Sandy would say, getting her homework done, but Emily liked to daydream. Once she started daydreaming, she would start doodling on her paper. Then, once she started doodling, she would have to throw her paper away because it didn't look nice and neat like her teachers liked it.

Sandy had told her to get her homework done. She said that she would give her an hour to figure things out or ask questions. She even sat with Emily, waiting to help. "Time's up," her stepmom said an hour later. "I need to do some chores." Sandy stood to go do the laundry.

"You're not my real mom, anyway," Emily said as she stormed off to her room.

Now, Emily sat at her desk with homework she didn't know how to do. Her stepmom had given her enough time to ask questions, but she had played around instead of working. Emily knew it was her fault. Tears streamed down her face.

Another hour went by as Emily sat in her bedroom trying to write an "I'm sorry" note. Normally, she drew hearts and flowers using all kinds of different colors, but this note was different. She knew she had to say sorry to Sandy for disobeying. Emily felt terrible. She loved her stepmom and wanted her to know it.

A knock on her bedroom made Emily jump. "Come in."

"How's your homework coming?" Sandy asked.

"I do have a couple of questions, but I want you to read something first." Emily handed her stepmom the note.

"What's this?" Sandy opened the card.

"I'M SORRY. I LOVE YOU!" was all it said.

Sandy hugged Emily tight.
"I forgive you. And I love you too."

I'm Sorry.
I Love You!

Your Turn

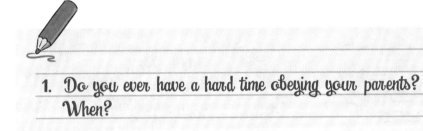

1. Do you ever have a hard time obeying your parents? When?

2. Because you don't always obey your parents, do you ever wonder if your parents still love you? If God still loves you?

17

Bible Story

The Boy Jesus at the Temple
Read Luke 2:41-52

Find the Missing Word

Mary treasured all these things in her ___ ___ ___ ___ ⃝.

1

Write About It

When was the last time you told your parents you loved them?

Tiny Treasure

God wants you to love him and obey what the Bible says.

Prayer

Lord God, thank you for my family. I know you chose them just for me. In Jesus' name, amen.

Do It!

Just as Jesus obeyed his earthly parents, you need to obey your parents, too. When you obey your parents, you are showing God's love! Let's show love to our parents by making them a card. It could be a few words on a piece of notebook paper or you can make a fancier card. Try this shiny heart card.

Shiny Heart Card

What You Need

- Colored construction paper

- Aluminum foil

- Scissors

- Glue stick

What You Do

1. Cut construction paper into a rectangle and fold in half to make a card.

2. Cut a heart out of aluminum foil. The easiest way is to fold a small piece of foil in half and then cut out half the heart along the fold.

3. Glue the foil heart to the front of the card. Gently smooth out the foil.

4. Write a nice message to your parent inside your card.

5. Hand the card to your parent, or place it somewhere they will find it as a surprise.

God Provides a Way

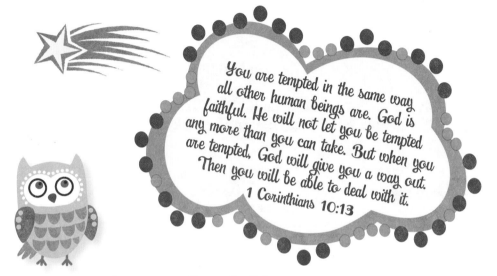

> You are tempted in the same way all other human beings are. God is faithful. He will not let you be tempted any more than you can take. But when you are tempted, God will give you a way out. Then you will be able to deal with it.
> 1 Corinthians 10:13

Too Much of a Good Thing

"Thanks for inviting me to your party, and for the candy, too," Brianna said to her friend Hannah as she climbed into her mom's car.

Hannah waved goodbye. "See you Monday at school. Thanks for the necklace." She ran on the sidewalk beside the now moving car. "And thanks for coming!"

Brianna looked into her candy bag. Her mouth watered as she saw many of her favorite treats. She couldn't wait to get home and eat some candy.

"How was the party?" Mom asked.

"Great!" Brianna closed the bag so her mom wouldn't see what was inside. "She got a lot of cool gifts. I especially liked the heart-shaped necklace I gave her."

 "I know your birthday is in a couple of weeks. Is that a hint?" Mom asked.

"You catch on quick, Mom." Brianna smiled.

Ten minutes later they pulled into their driveway. Mom said, "Dad wants you to help him in the backyard in a little while."

"All right, I'll be in my room." Brianna darted across the front lawn and into the house.

"Ah, time for candy," she whispered to herself as she dumped the contents of the bag onto her bed. Brianna organized her candy into groups: chocolate bars, hard candy, taffy. They all looked good. One piece, two pieces, three . . .

Brianna's trashcan was filling up with wrappers. "Just one more," she said to herself time and again as she popped yet another piece of candy into her mouth.

"Brianna!" She heard her mom call from the stairway. "Dad needs you in the backyard. NOW."

Brianna doubled over in pain. She couldn't believe she had eaten all the candy she received from the party. She didn't know why she did it, beside the fact that she has a "sweet tooth" as her mom would say. Why couldn't she just resist the sugary treats? What was it about chocolate bars and fruit-flavored morsels that made her forget how her stomach would feel afterward? Next time, she would take only one . . . or two.

"Mom," Brianna called out. "Mom!" she called again.

Mom peeked her head into her room. "What is it?"

"I don't feel so good." Brianna pointed to her trashcan.

Mom came in, looked inside the trashcan and knew the reason for her stomachache. "Oh, Brianna. I think next time I will hide the bag so that you won't be tempted to eat it all at once."

"Thanks, Mom," Brianna said.

Your Turn

1. Do you ever find yourself tempted by something? What do you do to not give in? Or do you just go with it?

2. What does today's verse mean when it says you won't be tempted "any more than you can take?"

Bible Story

The Temptation of Jesus
Read Luke 4:1-13

Find the Missing Word

Jesus was tempted in the desert for ___ ___ ◯ ___ ___ days.

6

Write About It

Write about a time when you were tempted to do something wrong.

Write five things you can do to escape when faced with temptation.

Tiny Treasure

God will provide a way out!

Prayer

Lord God, thank you for not letting me be tempted more than I can take. Thank you for always showing me a way out. In Jesus' name, amen.

Do It!

Just as God provided a way out for Jesus when he was tempted, he will provide a way out for you. Let's practice.

Run! Run around the block as fast as you can. Take a sibling, friend, or parent with you and tell them how you are going to flee temptation with God's help.

Or, try this fun game.

Temptation Tag

What You Need

• 2 or more players

What You Do

One person is "It" or the temptation. That player needs to catch the other player(s) before they touch a safety base you decide on (a tree, safety cone, trash can, etc.). The safety base represents freedom from temptation or a way out. Don't let temptation catch you!

When "It" touches another player, that player takes a turn to be "It."

God's Reward

Love your enemies. Do good to them. Lend to them without expecting to get anything back. Then you will receive a lot in return. And you will be children of the Most High God. He is kind to people who are evil and are not thankful.

LUKE 6:35

Loving When It's Tough

Jessica ran out the front door to ride her skateboard and noticed her new neighbor, Alyssa, playing with a tennis ball in front of Alyssa's house. Jessica had had a few run-ins with her neighbor already and decided they wouldn't exactly be best friends.

Jessica tried to be calm as she rode her skateboard up and down the sidewalk, but having to pass her neighbor's house made her hands sweat. Jessica decided the best way to face her neighbor was by talking with her.

"Hi." Jessica kicked her skateboard up and caught it with her right hand.

"Are you talking to me?" Alyssa asked.

"Yes." Jessica fidgeted with her skateboard wheels.

"You know," Alyssa said. "Skateboarding is for boys."

"You want to try?" Jessica asked, hoping to find something they could do together. "It's really fun."

 "No way." Alyssa shook her head. "You look like a boy wearing those ripped jeans and that T-shirt."

Jessica's eyes stung. She grabbed her skateboard and ran to her house. She threw her helmet and skateboard in the garage and ran to her bedroom, letting the tears stream down her face. She was hoping to get along with Alyssa, but after this . . . No way! Name calling hurt. How could she ever look Alyssa in the eye again?

 As Jessica lay on her bed, she remembered the first day her foster brother came to live with them. He was a noisy toddler and was frequently found in her bedroom playing with her things. Her mother told her to love him and be nice to him even when she didn't feel like it.

A plan began to form in Jessica's mind. What if she were super nice to Alyssa no matter what Alyssa did or said?

"Jessica," Mom called. "Come set the table for dinner."

After dinner, Jessica spotted the leftover dessert. "Hey, Mom, can I bring some brownies over to our new neighbors?"

Mom glanced at the clock. "Sure, but hurry home."

"OK, I will." Jessica placed four brownies on a paper plate.

Once at Alyssa's door, Jessica had second thoughts. "I'm asking for it," she said to herself as she rang the bell.

"Oh, hello, Mrs. Thompson. Is Alyssa home?" Jessica's voice shook.

"Yes, hold on a minute." A few seconds later, Alyssa appeared at the door.

Jessica wanted to run, but instead said, "Here, my mom made some

brownies. I thought you would like some." There, she did it.
No matter what, she felt good about giving Alyssa the brownies.

"Really?" Alyssa asked. "You would give me brownies after the way
I treated you?"

"Yeah," Jessica said, hopeful of a new friendship.

"Thanks." Alyssa smiled and took a big bite of a brownie.
"Hmm, they're good!"

Your Turn

1. Do you have friendly neighbors? What are some ways
   you can be a good neighbor?

2. Why do you think God wants to reward you for loving
   your enemies?

Bible Story

The Parable of the
Good Samaritan
Read Luke 10:25-37

Find the Missing Word

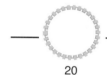

——— ◯ —— —— your neighbor as yourself.

20

Write About It

Who is someone you have a hard time being around?
Write about it here.

List ways you can follow the example of the Good Samaritan and be a good neighbor.

Tiny Treasure

God will reward you!

Prayer

Lord God, thank you for rewarding your children for helping others. Help me to love my enemies and do good to them. In Jesus' name, amen.

Do It!

Just as the Good Samaritan showed mercy to the hurt Jewish man, we are to do the same for others. Try baking these brownies with a parent and giving them to a new or difficult neighbor!

Jessica's Delicious Brownies

What You Need

- 9x13-inch baking pan
- 1 cup butter or margarine
- 2 cups granulated sugar
- 4 eggs
- 1½ cups all-purpose flour
- 1 teaspoon baking powder

- ½ teaspoon salt
- 12 tablespoons cocoa
- 2 teaspoons vanilla extract

Optional:

- 1 cup chopped nuts
- Confectioners sugar

What You Do

1. Preheat oven to 350°F.
2. Melt butter in baking pan on stove. Remove from heat. Stir in sugar; then eggs.
3. Sift and add flour, baking powder, salt, and cocoa. Mix in vanilla extract.
4. Optional: Add nuts, if desired.
5. Bake for 30 minutes.
6. Cool.
7. Optional: Sprinkle with confectioners' sugar, if desired. Enjoy!

God Will Guide

> I will guide you and teach you the way you should go. I will give you good advice and watch over you with love.
> Psalm 32:8

Help! What Is the Better Choice?

Savannah was on her way to school when her mom announced that they'd be going to Aunt Lisa's house for the weekend. Savannah wanted to scream, "NO!" Yesterday, she had received an invitation from her friend Rachel for a party on Saturday.

The party was going to be at the rock-climbing gym, something Savannah had always wanted to do. She grabbed her backpack, unzipped the front pocket and glanced at the invitation. Why didn't she give it to her mom yesterday?

All day long her stomach was in knots. The trip to Aunt Lisa's house was going to be a family reunion. She knew the trip was important, but Rachel was her best friend in the whole world. She had a decision to make—disappoint Rachel or her family. Savannah didn't know what to do.

"What's the matter, Savannah?" her mom asked when Savannah hopped in the van after school. "You don't look happy."

"Oh, just a hard day." Savannah put on her seatbelt.

"Hard in what way?" her mom probed.

"I've got a decision to make and I don't know what to do." Savannah hoped her mom wouldn't ask any more questions.

33

"Well, do you want to share with me, and I'll see if I can help you?" Mom asked.

"Not really," Savannah said, "I think I need to work this one out on my own."

"OK," Mom said. "Just remember I'm here for you if you need me."

After pulling into the driveway, Savannah got out of the van and ran to her favorite thinking tree. As Savannah climbed, she remembered something her mom would often say, "If you need an answer to a problem, talk to God in prayer."

Savannah held onto the branch very tightly as she closed her eyes. "Dear God, please help me to know what is the right thing to do. You know Rachel is my best friend. I don't want to hurt her feelings by not going to her party. But I also don't want to hurt my family! Show me what to do. In Jesus' name, amen." Savannah sighed . . . and smiled, suddenly knowing the answer.

After Savannah retrieved the invitation from her backpack, she handed it to her mom.

"What's this?"

"An invitation from Rachel," Savannah said.

"Wow, rock climbing. That sounds fun," Mom said as she read the invitation.

"I decided to go with you to Aunt Lisa's instead," Savannah said, proud of her decision.

"Savannah, that is very thoughtful of you," Mom said, "but Aunt Lisa called while you were at school and said this weekend wouldn't work because she has the flu. I appreciate your willingness to go even though I know you'd rather be with your friend Rachel. It looks like the party is going to work out."

"Yeessss!" Savannah shouted as she jumped in the air.

Your Turn

1. When is a time it was hard for you to make a decision? What helped you make your decision?

2. What are ways God can help you discover the right thing to do?

Bible Story

At the Home of Mary and Martha
Read Luke 10:38-42

Find the Missing Word

Mary sat at Jesus' ___ ___ ⎯◯⎯ ___ , listening to what he
was saying.

3

Write About It

Do you relate more to Mary or Martha in the Bible Story? Why?

Tell about a time you made a good decision because you asked God to help you.

Tiny Treasure

God will guide you!

Prayer

Lord God, thank you for watching and guiding me. Help me to make good decisions. In Jesus' name, amen.

Do It!

Just as Mary made the better choice by sitting at Jesus' feet, with God as your guide, you can make good decisions, too.

We can learn so much from our parents and grandparents. Why don't you ask one of them to tell you a life story about a time they made a good choice with God's help? And . . .

Take this Decision Quiz

1. When your mom asks you to do your homework, do you:

    a. Complain that you don't want to do your homework.

    b. Sigh loudly, then grab your backpack and sit at the table.

    c. Get to it right away. The quicker you start, the sooner you'll be finished.

2. Your best friend wants to hang out with the new girl at recess. Do you:

    a. Tell your friend you only want to play with her and no one else.

    b. Invite the new girl to eat lunch with you and your friend.

    c. Find someone else to play with.

3. It's quiet reading time at school. Do you:

    a. Get your book out and read quietly.

    b. Daydream.

    c. Write your friend a note because she's having a bad day.

4. You're spending the night at a friend's house and she wants to watch a movie you know your parents wouldn't approve. Do you:

    a. Watch it anyway, but close your eyes at the bad parts.

    b. Call your parents and ask if you can watch it.

    c. Tell your friend that you'd rather watch something else.

5. You go outside and see a bike tipped over and a child crying. Do you:

    a. Run to the child and see if you can help.

    b. Look away and go back inside your house. The child's mom will hear and come running.

    c. Ask a sibling to help the child.

What Is the Best Choice?

Use the key below to score your answers.

    1a. Ignoring your mom's request is never a good choice because it is putting your wants before being obedient. Give yourself 1 point.

    b. Being slow to listen but still obeying is second best. Give yourself 3 points.

    c. The best choice is listening to your mom right away. Give yourself 5 points.

    2a. Telling your friend you only want to play with her and no one else is never a good choice because that is being selfish. Give yourself 1 point.

    b. The best choice was to invite the new girl to eat lunch with you and your friends. Give yourself 5 points.

    c. Finding someone else to play with is second best because you are allowing your friend to play with the new girl. Give yourself 3 points.

3a. The best choice was getting your book out and reading quietly. Give yourself 5 points.

b. Writing your friend a note is OK as long as you sit quietly. Give yourself 3 points.

c. Daydreaming in class is never a good choice because it isn't doing your best. Give yourself 1 point.

4a. Watching a movie you know your parents don't approve of is never a good idea. Give yourself 1 point.

b. The best choice was calling your parents and asking them if you could watch the movie because you are being mindful of your parent's rules. Give yourself 5 points.

c. Telling your friend that you'd rather watch something else is showing you can make a good decision on your own. Give yourself 3 points.

5a. The best choice was not being afraid to help others in need. Give yourself 5 points.

b. Looking away is never a good choice when you can do something to help. Give yourself 1 point.

c. Telling a sibling to help is at least being concerned about the crying child. Give yourself 3 points.

Tally Your Score

20–25 points – Wonderful! Keep up the good work! You know how to make good choices.

15–20 points – Good. There is always room for improvement.

Less than 15 – Ask God to help you make better choices.

Making a good decision is tough! There are some days you will make better choices than other days. Take one day at a time and pray for God to guide you.

God Is Light

The Lord is my light, and he saves me. Why should I fear anyone?
Psalm 27:1

Better Late than Never

Jessica hugged her soccer ball as her mom drove her to soccer practice. "Does practice end early today?" Mom asked.

"Same time," Jessica said. "Remember this Saturday is our last game and it's our turn to bring the snacks."

"Oh, that's right. I'll run to the grocery store." Mom pulled up to the soccer field.

"After Saturday, I won't see Savannah very much." Jessica frowned. "I wish we went to the same school. I only see her at soccer practice."

"We can always invite her over sometime," Mom said.

"I'll get her phone number." Jessica opened the car door. "Bye, Mom. Oh, remember I'm getting a ride home with Savannah's mom."

Practice started on time as usual. Jessica was on her second lap around the field when she noticed Savannah getting dropped off. If Jessica was ever going to get up the nerve to invite Savannah to church, now was the time. Jessica really wanted Savannah to know Jesus.

She was trying to think of something to say as Savannah caught up to her on the last lap around the field. "Hi," Savannah said. "I'm late again!

"Better late than never," Jessica said. They both started giggling. Jessica knew this was her chance to talk to Savannah. "Hey, remember I told you how Sundays were family days?" Jessica asked.

"Yeah," Savannah said.

"Well, it's because we go to church and learn about God." Jessica's breaths came out in short bursts as they made their final turn around the field.

"Oh," Savannah said. "What's that like?"

Jessica said a quick prayer. "It's great. We sing some songs, learn a Bible story, and then talk about it. I really like going because I want to know God better."

"Sounds cool," Savannah said.

Jessica grabbed her soccer ball as their coach announced the next drill. "Let's be partners," Jessica said, hoping to finish their conversation.

"OK," Savannah said.

After a few kicks of the soccer ball back and forth, Savannah said, "I don't think my parents believe in God."

"Well, do you want to go to church with me this Sunday?" Jessica stopped the ball with her right foot.

"I'd like that," Savannah said. "Let me ask my mom when she picks us up."

"Line up for the scrimmage," the coach called to the group of girls.

Jessica and Savannah joined the coach and all the girls to find out their positions. The next hour flew by.

"Mom," Jessica called as she ran into the house after practice.

"I finally did it!"

"Did what?" Mom smiled at Jessica's excitement.

"I invited Savannah to church. She asked her mom on the drive home if she could come this Sunday . . . and her Mom said yes! You know what? Inviting her wasn't as scary as I thought it would be."

Your Turn

1. Do you ever invite your friends to church? Is it easy or hard?

2. What does the verse mean when it says that God is our light and that we don't need to feel fear?

Bible Story

Salt and Light
Read Matthew 5:13-16

Find the Missing Word

A ___ ___ ___ ◯ gives light to everyone in the house.

11

Write About It

What does it mean to let your light shine? How do you let your light shine?

Tell about a time that you talked to a friend about Jesus.

Tiny Treasure

God is our light and salvation!

Prayer

Lord God, thank you for being my light and my salvation. I know I don't need to fear telling others about you. In Jesus' name, amen.

Do It!

Just as Jesus told his disciples they need to be salt and light, you too, can be salt and light by sharing the good news of Jesus. Try this salty science experiment to see how salt and light work together.

Salt Crystal Garden

What You Need

- 3 clean dry sponges

- Aluminum pie plate

- Glass measuring cup

- ¼ cup of table salt

- ¼ cup of water

- ¼ cup of laundry bluing (Bluing can be bought by the bottle at the grocery store under the brand name of Mrs. Stewart's Laundry Bluing.)

- 2 tablespoons of household ammonia

- Mixing bowl

- Metal spoon

- Food coloring, blue and green

- 1 cup chopped nuts

- Confectioners sugar

What You Do

1. Arrange the three sponges in the pie plate.

2. Pour the salt, water, bluing, and ammonia into the mixing bowl and stir to mix well.

3. Pour this mixture over the sponges and then spoon out the rest of the thick portion, spreading it evenly over the sponges.

4. Sprinkle drops of blue and green food coloring randomly on the sponges.

5. Let the pan sit. It may take hours or even days to see results.

6. Try placing a heat lamp over the salt garden to see if it grows faster.

7. Note observations.

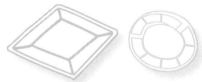

What Happened?

The crystals grew due to the liquid evaporating into the air. The molecules in this liquid are made up of atoms. When the liquid evaporates, the remaining atoms will pack together to form crystals. The time that it takes for this to happen will depend on how quickly the water evaporates.

God's Unseen Riches

We don't spend all our time looking at what we can see. Instead, we look at what we can't see. That's because what can be seen lasts only a short time. But what can't be seen will last forever.
2 Corinthians 4:18

Thinking of Others

"Savannah," Dad called. "Time to go shopping."

A big smile crossed Savannah's face. She enjoyed shopping with her dad because he usually bought her something cool. "Coming," She ran down the stairs.

Once at the mall, Savannah noticed some people were sitting in front with sleeping bags and shopping carts full of stuff. "Why are they sitting there?"

"Because they are homeless," Dad said.

"What does that mean?" Savannah asked.

"They don't have a home anymore," Dad said. "They might have lost their jobs, or didn't have enough money to pay their rent. There are many reasons why people become homeless. Remember last year when our house caught fire and we had to stay in a hotel for a while until it was rebuilt?"

Savannah nodded.

"In a way, we were homeless then too," Dad said. Savannah grabbed her dad's hand and squeezed it tight.

As they entered the mall, Savannah's eyes widened as she saw all the fun stores she wanted to go into. Her dad let her buy an outfit and shoes, too.

After shopping for a couple of hours, Dad offered to buy hot chocolates at the coffee shop. "Yum, this is good, Dad," Savannah said, careful not to spill her hot drink. "Thanks for the shopping trip. I really enjoy spending time with my favorite dad."

"You're welcome." Dad smiled.

Once home, Savannah ran to her room to try on her new outfit. She couldn't wait to wear it to school the next day. She hoped her friends would notice and compliment her.

Flipping on some music, Savannah danced while watching herself in the mirror. After a few songs, Savannah sat by her computer, staring at the blank screen. She was really happy with all that she had, but she couldn't help thinking about the homeless people she saw at the mall. Sad feelings came over her as she looked around her room, remembering what it was like to have it all taken away.

There were a couple of things Savannah knew she couldn't live without. First, there was "Fuzzy," her childhood teddy bear. She picked him up and stroked his soft head. Because of the fire, Fuzzy was one of the only things she had since she was a baby. The second thing she couldn't live without was a recent picture of her family. She always kept it in a ceramic frame by her bed.

As the next song ended, Savannah had an idea. She started making a pile of toys she didn't play with anymore. Savannah put the toys in a box and marked "For homeless children."

"Hey, Dad," Savannah said, carrying a heaping box full of toys down the stairs. "I want to give these toys to the homeless children!"

"Great idea," Dad said, hurrying over to help her with the box. "I'm so proud of you!"

Your Turn

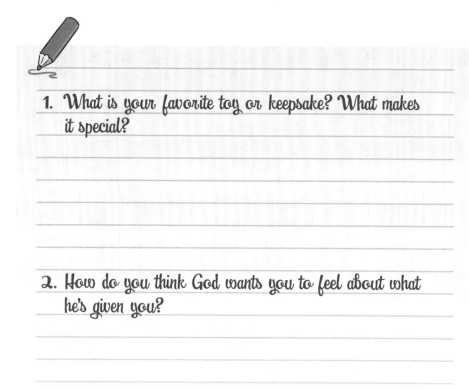

1. What is your favorite toy or keepsake? What makes it special?

2. How do you think God wants you to feel about what he's given you?

Bible Story

Treasures in Heaven
Read Matthew 6:19-24

Find the Missing Word

The ___ ___ ___ is the lamp of the body.

Write About It

Can you think of a time when you bought something and then discovered it wasn't as cool as you thought?

What do you treasure? What could you give away?

Tiny Treasure

God looks at your heart.

Prayer

Lord God, help me to focus on things that are important to you. Help me to treasure those things that are eternal and not earthly things. In Jesus' name, amen.

Do It!

Jesus told his disciples that they must treasure things that can't be seen, but are eternal. This is often referred to as storing up treasures in heaven. You can store up treasures in heaven, too!

Some examples of heavenly treasures are:

- Putting your relationship with God first

- Spending time with family and friends

- Showing kindness to others

- Being a cheerful giver

- Serving God by serving others

- Sharing God's Word

Here is crafty idea to make with things that remind you of heavenly treasures.

Heavenly Treasures Box

What You Need

- Marker or paint pen

- Sturdy cardboard box and lid (shoe box, small electronics box, etc.)

- White glue

- Decorations and keepsakes: wrapping paper, photos of family and friends, drawings, special birthday or holiday cards or anything else that reminds you of eternal things, heavenly treasures.

- Water

- Paint brush

What You Do

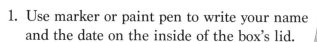

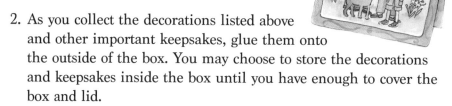

1. Use marker or paint pen to write your name and the date on the inside of the box's lid.

2. As you collect the decorations listed above and other important keepsakes, glue them onto the outside of the box. You may choose to store the decorations and keepsakes inside the box until you have enough to cover the box and lid.

3. To give the box a durable finish, thin glue with water. Brush the thinned glue all over the box and lid. Set aside to dry. When the glue dries, the coating will be clear.

Treasure Tip

This clever treasure box may have enough room for your Bible, a stack of memory verses, ideas for service, or even a tiny book of best friends' autographs.

God Takes Care of Every Need

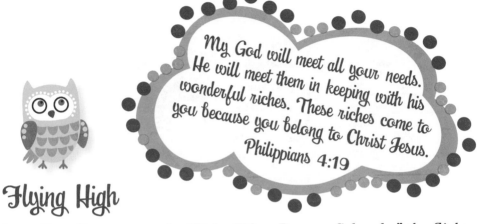

My God will meet all your needs. He will meet them in keeping with his wonderful riches. These riches come to you because you belong to Christ Jesus.
Philippians 4:19

Flying High

"Boarding all passengers for Flight 209 to Denver, Colorado," the flight attendant said.

"Time to board." Dad smiled.

As the family gathered their belongings, Brianna's stomach clenched. She had looked forward to going to camp with her family, but now she was having second thoughts.

They found their seats right behind first class and the curtain that separated the front from the back of the plane.

"Here, let me put your bag in the overhead bin," Dad said.

"OK, but let me get my book first," Brianna said.

Once they were up in the air and the flight attendants gave the emergency information, Brianna turned toward her mom. "How long before we get there?"

"It's a two-hour flight to Denver," Mom said.

Brianna let out a big sigh. She had only flown once before to Grandma and Grandpa's house. She forgot the weird feelings flying did to her stomach, but then again, she might have butterflies from the upcoming camp they were going to attend. What if no one liked her? What if the food tasted gross? What if the bed was uncomfortable?

55

 She had so many thoughts swirling in her head.

Soon the flight attendant came down the aisle with drinks for everyone.

"Excited about camp?" Dad asked.

Brianna hesitated. "I guess so."

"It's been the only thing you've talked about for months," Mom said. "Are you nervous?"

 "Maybe a little." Brianna took a sip of her soft drink.

"I know you'll make lots of new friends," Dad said.

"You think so?"

"I know so."

Soon the flight attendant came back to gather everyone's trash.

"Mom and I will be attending some of the adult workshops, but we'll be available if you or Elizabeth need us," Dad said.

"I have a feeling you'll have so much fun that you won't care where we are." Mom grinned.

Dad reached into his jacket pocket and pulled out a piece of paper. "Why don't you take a look at this brochure and read all about what we're going to do this week."

"All right," Brianna said, feeling comforted by her parents' concern.

"And remember, God will meet all your needs, so you don't need to worry," Mom said.

Brianna read the brochure cover to cover and was once again getting excited about the camp and the week's adventure. She closed her eyes and took a nap for the remainder of the flight, dreaming of kids she was soon going to meet.

Your Turn

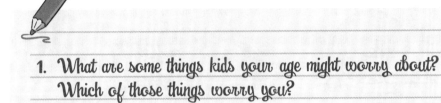

1. What are some things kids your age might worry about? Which of those things worry you?

2. How can knowing that God will take care of you help you not to worry?

57

Bible Story

Do Not Worry

Read Matthew 6:25-34

Find the Missing Word

Seek first his ___ ___ ___ ___ ◯ ___ ___ , and his

18

righteousness and all these things will be given to you.

Write About It

Think about a time when you worried about something. What helped you feel better?

Since we can't add a single hour to our lives by worrying, what should we do instead?

Tiny Treasure

God takes care of your every need.

Prayer

Lord God, thank you for meeting all my needs. Help me not to worry, but to trust in YOU. In Jesus' name, amen.

Do It!

Just as Jesus taught his disciples that they do not need to worry about tomorrow, you too, can learn not to worry because God will meet all your needs.

One of the best ways to express ourselves is through music. Try writing a song! Here is an easy way to do it. Find some songs that you love and replace the words with words of your own. Make each line the EXACT same length and make your rhyme pattern follow the one in the existing song. Here's an example: Sing the following words to the tune of "Mary Had a Little Lamb."

> God will meet all of your needs,
> All your needs, all your needs
> God will meet all of your needs,
> For he'll take care of you!

Now it's your turn!

Try using "Mary Had a Little Lamb" or another simple song such as "Twinkle, Twinkle Little Star" or "London Bridge."

God Gives Good Gifts

> Every good and perfect gift is from God. This kind of gift comes down from the Father who created the heavenly lights. These lights create shadows that move. But the Father does not change like these shadows.
>
> James 1:17

Drumming to the Right Beat

"Lauren!" Mom called. "Can you please stop drumming on your desk? I can hear you all the way downstairs!"

"It helps me do my math," Lauren called back, adding numbers to the beat of her hands hitting the edge of the desk.

The next thing she knew, Lauren heard a knock on her door. "Lauren?"

"Come in." Lauren knew what was coming next. She was in trouble.

"I know you like to drum on everything you see," Mom said. "That is why I've decided to give you these." Mom held something up.

"No way!" Lauren exclaimed. "My very own drumsticks!"

"Yes," Mom said, "But before I give these to you, we need to set some rules."

"Anything." Lauren beamed at the new gift.

"First of all, only drum downstairs."

"You mean on Dad's old set in the basement?" Lauren asked.

"Yes," said her mom, "Dad can't seem to part with that old drum set, so you can use it."

"All right!" Lauren grinned.

"I just called the music pastor from our church and he has agreed to give you some free lessons after church on Sundays. So, for rule number two," Mom said. "You need to practice."

"Yes, I sure will." Lauren rubbed her hands together as if she were ready to practice right then.

"OK, and third." Mom gave her a stern look. "You need to stop drumming when I tell you to."

Lauren couldn't wait to get her hands on the drumsticks. "Deal!"

Mom handed the drumsticks to Lauren. "I think God has given you the gift of rhythm and I can't wait to hear you play those drums, so go downstairs and try them out!"

"Thank you!" Lauren loved the way the drumsticks felt in her hands as she raced downstairs.

Your Turn

1. What talents do you have? If you're not sure, think about things that you enjoy doing.

2. What are some of the different talents and gifts God gives his children?

TRAVELING

FOREING LANGUAGE STUDY

MUSIC PLAYING

BIKING

PAINTING

Bible Story

Ask, Seek, Knock
Read Matthew 7:7-12

Find the Missing Word

The ___ ⃝ ___ ___ will be opened if we knock.

5

Write About It

Tell about a time that you were complimented for something you'd done. (For example: writing, art, sports, drawing, music, etc.) Your ability to do a good job at that likely began with a gift from God. Practicing that talent helped you get better at it.

List some ways you can use your gifts and talents for God.

Tiny Treasure

God's gifts make you special.

Prayer

Lord God, thank you for giving me good gifts. Help me to use my talents for your glory. In Jesus' name, amen.

Do It!

The Bible says our Father gives good gifts to those who ask him. That means you can ask God to give you good gifts. All you need to do is ask, seek, and knock. Try making this cool sign to hang on a door. It will remind you of this promise.

Ask, Seek, Knock Door Hanger

What You Need

- 12-inch length of cord or yarn

- Tacky glue

- 7 jumbo colored craft sticks

- 1 standard craft stick

- Adhesive-backed craft-foam shapes

Optional
- Markers

What You Do

1. Tie a knot at each end of the 12-inch length of cord or string. Glue the knots to each end of a jumbo craft stick. Glue a second jumbo craft stick on top, sandwiching the cord between the jumbo craft stick.

2. To make door hanger, glue the sandwiched craft sticks at the top of the standard craft stick. Glue five more jumbo craft sticks close to the sandwiched sticks.

3. Place a heavy book on top of door hanger. While the door hanger glue dries, search the craft-foam letters to find the letters in the words "ask," "seek," and "knock."

4. Peel paper off the back of craft-foam letters and arrange on the door hanger to read "Ask, Seek, Knock."

5. Use craft-foam shapes or markers to add decorative touches.

God Rocks

The LORD lives! Give praise to my Rock! Give honor to my God, the Rock! He is my Savior!
2 Samuel 22:47

Lean on Me

"Hi, Mom," Brianna said when she got home from school on the worst day of her life.

"Hi there, anything new happen at school today?" Mom asked.

"Not much." Brianna looked into the pantry for a snack. She took out the crackers and put them on the counter, then opened the refrigerator. Heaving a big sigh, Brianna grabbed a slice of cheese and an apple.

"Since it's Friday, do you want to call a friend to come over?" Mom asked.

"No way!" exclaimed Brianna, cutting into her apple with a knife.

"Uh, Brianna, maybe I should do that," Mom said. "Something seems to be bothering you."

"Everything is fine, Mom," Brianna fibbed. "I just want to watch TV and be by myself," grabbed her snack and left the kitchen.

Brianna turned on the TV. Nothing good was on, but she didn't care. She just wanted to forget about her day at school. But it wasn't working.

Brianna turned the volume up, hoping she could get into the television show.

Mom entered the family room. "Whoa, way too loud."

Brianna turned the sound down and scowled at her mom.

"OK," Mom said. "Turn off the TV. We need to talk."

Brianna folded her arms across her chest. She didn't want to talk to Mom and Mom couldn't make her!

"Brianna," Mom said. "Something happened at school today that I wish you would tell me about."

Brianna sat starring at the now blank TV screen. Her mom didn't need to know everything, did she?

"Your teacher called me, Brianna. She knows what happened. She overheard your friends at recess teasing you," Mom said.

"Some friends."

Mom sat beside her. "You do have a friend who will always be with you. You know that, don't you?"

"Yes. I know," Brianna nodded. Brianna knew that God was always on her side, no matter what. "But it hurts just the same."

"I know it hurts, honey," Mom said. "Friendships come and go, but God will always be with you."

'I guess I'll have to make some new friends." Brianna nibbled on her cheese.

"Your teacher also told me was that she was going to keep those girls in during recess on Monday to clean the classroom and write you an apology note. I think everything will turn out just fine." Mom smiled.

Brianna decided to write in her journal and talk to the one friend she knew would always be there for her—God.

Your Turn

1. Who is someone in your life you can always lean on?

2. Our verse says that God is your Rock. What does that mean to you?

Bible Story

The Wise and Foolish Builders

Read Matthew 7:24-27

Find the Missing Word

The __ __ __ ◯ __ did not fall because it had its foundation on the rock.

10

Write About It

What was the difference between the wise and the foolish builder in the Bible story?

71

List ways you can build your life on God, your firm foundation.

Tiny Treasure

God wants you to lean on him!

Prayer

Lord God, thank you for being my constant Rock! Help me to lean on you. In Jesus' name, amen.

Do It!

Just as the wise man built his house on the rock, you too, can build your life on a firm foundation. Try making this recipe for rock candy to remind you of God, your Rock.

 Rock Candy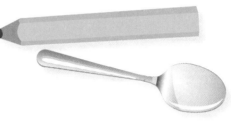

What You Need

- 1 cup water
- Glass or enamel saucepan
- 2 cups sugar
- Large spoon or spatula
- String
- Pencil
- Glass

What You Do

1. Put the water in saucepan and bring to a boil. Turn off heat.

2. Slowly add sugar, stirring to dissolve. Keep adding sugar until no more will dissolve. Allow to cool.

3. While it cools, tie a short piece of string to a pencil and lay the pencil across the glass so the string hangs down into the glass.

4. When the sugar water is cool, pour it into the glass and put it where it won't be disturbed for several days. Watch for sugar crystals to form. They will grow larger if left alone for a few days.

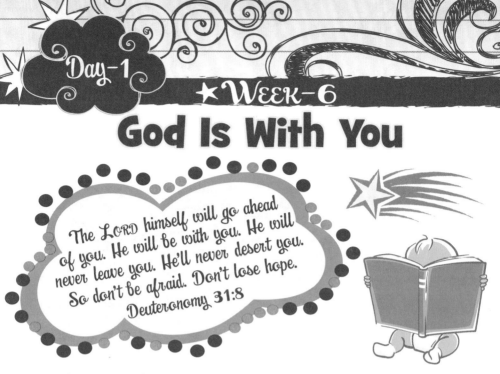

God Is With You

The LORD himself will go ahead of you. He will be with you. He will never leave you. He'll never desert you. So don't be afraid. Don't lose hope.
Deuteronomy 31:8

A Picture Is Worth a Thousand Words

Savannah ate breakfast with a frown. Today was the day her class needed to bring baby pictures for a project at school. Savannah didn't have one baby picture. The earliest picture she had was when she was ten years old. Savannah knew she would have to explain to her teacher and friends the reason. Last year, her house caught fire and most everything burned—including her toys, clothes, and all her baby pictures.

After breakfast, Savannah ran upstairs to grab the photo by her bed. She stuffed it inside her backpack and ran outside to catch the bus. "Bye, Mom," she said over her shoulder.

The bus ride to school went by too quickly. Savannah sat in her usual seat by the window in the second to the last row in the back. A first grader sat down next to her, which seemed to be an annoying daily occurrence, but this morning she welcomed the sight of the brown-haired girl and her constant chatter.

As Savannah walked into class, she noticed kids already sharing their photos with each other. She could hear, "You were so cute!" and "Were you really that bald?" and "Wow, you were chubby!" Savannah glanced at her photo still in the ceramic frame.

"Oh, hi, Savannah," said Ben, Savannah's desk partner. "I'll show you my picture if you show me yours."

"Um, well, that's OK . . . I don't want to share mine yet." Savannah kept her photo hidden inside her backpack.

The bell rang.

The teacher stood in the front of the classroom with a picture in her hand.

"OK, everyone," Mrs. Turner said. "I'd like to share my photo first. This is a picture of me when I was two years old. That was back in the day when parents didn't take as many pictures as they do now. Another reason why I'm a little older in this photo is because my aunt and uncle raised me and adopted me into their family."

The room was silent as Mrs. Turner continued, "Adoption is one way families are made. Some children grow up with relatives, like me, and others live with stepparents. And some are blessed with wonderful parents that love them from birth."

Savannah had another reason why her earliest photo was taken last year. The fire. She shifted in her seat, hoping no one noticed how uncomfortable she felt.

"Now, there are a couple of kids in our class who don't have a baby picture to share," Mrs. Turner continued, "and I wanted to tell you my story so that you all of you feel comfortable sharing your stories."

Savannah noticed Ben raising his hand. Oh, boy, maybe he knows I don't have a baby picture and is going to announce it to the class!

"Yes, Ben," Mrs. Turner said. "Do you have a question?"

"Can I go to the bathroom?" Ben asked.

Everyone giggled.

"May I?" Mrs. Turner asked.

Ben nodded.

"Yes, you may." Mrs. Turner nodded.

Savannah sat quietly in her chair. She reached into her backpack and felt the ceramic frame surrounding her photo. She thought about what she learned in Sunday school a few weeks ago. Her teacher talked about a verse in the Old Testament that said she didn't need to be afraid or discouraged because God was with her and would never leave her.

"Who would like to share their picture now?" Mrs. Turner asked.

Savannah slowly raised her hand.

Her teacher smiled. "Savannah, you're first. Please come on up to the front of the class."

Your Turn

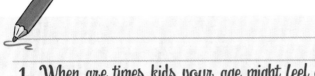

1. When are times kids your age might feel afraid? When have you felt afraid?

2. What does our verse mean when it says that God will never leave you nor forsake you? How can knowing this help when you feel afraid?

Bible Story

Jesus Calms
the Storm
Read Matthew 8:23-27

Find the Missing Word

Jesus got into the ___ ◯ ___ ___ and his disciples followed him

21

Write About It

Tell about a stormy time in your life when you were comforted to know God was with you.

How can you show your faith in God during difficult times?

Tiny Treasure

God will be with you wherever you go!

Prayer

Lord God, thank you for being with me at all times. Help me not to be afraid or discouraged. In Jesus' name, amen.

Do It!

Just as Jesus calmed the storm in our Bible story, he will calm the storms in your life, too. Try this interesting science experiment so that you remember God is with you always, even on the rainy days.

Making Rain

What You Need

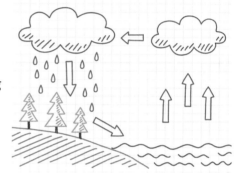

- Quart-sized resealable plastic bag

- Masking tape

- Food coloring

- Water

What You Do

1. Pour water into the plastic bag. Add a few drops of food coloring.

2. Seal the bag and place it in a sunny window.

3. Tape one corner of the top of the bag to the window.

4. Let the sun shine on the bag for a couple of hours, then observe what you see.

Just like the water from the Earth evaporates and returns back to Earth as precipitation, the sun heats the water and air sealed in the bag, causing the water to evaporate and clouds to form. When the clouds can't hold any more water, it starts to rain.

God Carries the Load

> Give praise to the Lord. Give praise to God our Savior. He carries our heavy loads day after day.
> Psalm 68:19

I'm Too Tired

Dear Secret Journal,

Here we go again . . . more questions about my mom. Will they ever end? At school, I could hear kids whisper to each other while looking in my direction. Maybe I'm just paranoid, but it feels like everyone wants to know how my mother died. Don't they know I have questions, too?

I've had dreams about my mom lately. I've pretended what life would be like if she were here. I miss her. I try to remember how she looked and what she smelled like, but it's been so long. One day she was on Earth and the next she was gone. It was all a bad nightmare. I'm glad my dad is still alive. He could have died in that car accident, too.

Anyway, I'm just tired of all the questions and confusion that is swirling around in my head. Why couldn't my mom just be alive? Life would have been so much easier.

It was really hard when my dad started dating Sandy. I know I wasn't being very nice, but I thought no one could replace my mom. My dad told me that Sandy wasn't replacing my mom, but that she was completing our family. He told me that there would be a time when I'd really need a mom, and that I would be glad Sandy is here.

He was right. I already feel that way, but sometimes I feel guilty—like I'm betraying my mom. It makes me feel yucky. Some days I don't think about my mom at all, and other days I think about her all day long. Today is just one of those days when I can't stop thinking about her.

I remember being a flower girl at my dad's wedding. People would look at me and shake their heads like they felt sorry for me. I thought it was supposed to be a happy day.

Sandy and my dad were gone for two weeks on a honeymoon. When they came back, Sandy and I had talks when she put me to bed. She did the best she could at answering my questions, but then one day she told me she doesn't understand everything either. Truth is, I'm glad Sandy came here when my mom couldn't take care of me anymore.

Yeah, sometimes we don't get along, but all kids are that way with their parents, right? At least that's what my friends say. And my friends really like my new mom too. They like to come over to my house when Sandy makes lasagna. Sometimes I get angry that I have a stepmom but mostly I'm OK about it. If my mom can't be with me, then I'm glad Sandy is. The best part is that my dad is happy.

I'm going to sign off. My brain hurts.

Emily

Emily closed her journal and slipped it underneath her mattress. She lay back against her pillow. She closed her eyes and prayed, "Dear God, I can't stop thinking about my mom today. I'm tired of all the questions. Help me to remember that you will carry my heavy loads. Amen."

"Emily," her stepmom called. "Time to set the table. Lasagna tonight!"

Emily smiled. "I'm coming!"

82

Your Turn

1. Is there something on your mind that you keep thinking about? What is it?

2. Our verse says God will take our "heavy loads" and give us peace. Heavy loads are things that weigh us down with worry or fear. Are there any "heavy loads" you would like to give to God? What will it feel like if you do?

Bible Story

Rest for the Weary
Read Matthew 11:25-30

Find the Missing Word

You will find ___ ___ ___ ___ for your soul.

Write About It

Tell about a time you felt tired of or worn out by something. What did you do about it?

Who can give you rest? How?

_____

_____

_____

_____

_____

Tiny Treasure

God understands your worries.

Prayer

Lord God, thank you for daily carrying my heavy loads. Help me to rest in you. In Jesus' name, amen.

Do It!

Jesus can give you rest. And there are things you can do to help you get the rest you need. On the next page is an acronym about rest. Follow the advice in this acronym to do your part to get needed rest. Make a poster of this acronym and hang it on your bedroom wall.

What You Need

- Markers or paint pens

- Sheet of poster board

Optional

- Stickers or adhesive-back craft-foam shapes

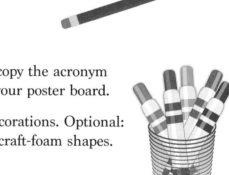

What You Do

- Use markers or paint pens to copy the acronym shown on the next page onto your poster board.

- Add additional drawings or decorations. Optional: Add stickers or adhesive-back craft-foam shapes.

Alternate Idea

Instead of making a poster of the acronym, write it on a 3x5-inch card and tape it to your bathroom mirror.

REST

R stands for Relationship

Restore your relationship with God
by reading your Bible every day.

E stands for Eat

Eat healthy! Try eating lots of fruits and vegetables.
Even our stomachs need a rest from junk food!

S stands for Sleep

Try going to bed just 15 minutes earlier than normal.
Sometimes it takes a while to fall asleep, so those
extra minutes will help.

T stands for Time out

Take a time out from your busy schedule. Setting time each
day to sit and relax can give you new energy to carry on.

★ WEEK-7

God's Faithfulness

> What the LORD says is right and true. He is faithful in everything he does.
>
> Psalm 33:4

Doing the Right Thing

At school, Jessica sat with her friends on the outdoor picnic table. Every day at recess, they would sit in the same place and trade snacks from their lunches. Jessica noticed a little girl who didn't have a snack. After looking at her more carefully, Jessica saw holes in her shoes and a tear in her jacket.

 "Hey, you guys," Jessica said to her friends Kayla and Taylor, "I wonder if that little girl needs food."

"I'm sure her friends will give her some," Kayla said.

"I don't know if she has any friends." Jessica kicked the dirt under the table with her right toe. "I never see her playing with anyone."

"She's at least two grades younger than us," said Kayla. "I wouldn't be seen with her."

"Yeah," Taylor said. "What would our friends think? Who cares about her anyway?"

Jessica didn't feel right about what her friends were saying. She took a bite of one of the cookies she and kept watching the little redheaded girl. Now two boys were picking on her.

"I'm going over to talk with her." Jessica jumped up from her spot at the picnic table. "I'll be right back."

Kayla and Taylor shrugged their shoulders, as if she was making a big mistake.

Jessica walked slowly to the little girl, hoping not to scare her. The two boys ran off when they noticed Jessica approach.

"Hi, there," Jessica said.

"Hi," the little girl said in a quiet voice.

"What's your name?" Jessica bent down a little to match the girl's height.

"Olivia."

"That's a very pretty name," Jessica said. "Want a cookie?" She reached into her sack lunch and pulled out a chocolate-chip cookie.

"Sure," Olivia said. "That's my favorite kind."

"Were those boys picking on you?" Jessica watched the little girl wolf down the cookie in only a few bites.

"Yeah," Olivia said. "They called me Carrots and pointed at the holes in my shoes."

"I think you are have pretty hair," Jessica said. "And I just outgrew some shoes that just might be your size. Do you think you might like them?"

Olivia shrugged. "Do you have another cookie?"

"No, but I can share my food with you during lunch." Jessica looked inside her bag. "I have a peanut butter and jelly sandwich, apple slices, and carrots."

A smile lit up the little girl's face. "OK, but no carrots. I hate carrots."

Jessica smiled, understanding the girl's meaning. "OK, no carrots."

Your Turn

1. Describe a time you did something because you knew it is the right thing to do. Was it easy to do the right thing, or was there something that made it difficult?

2. Our verse tells us that what God says is right and true. How can this change some of the decisions you make? How can you know what God says?

Bible Story

A Crippled Woman Healed on the Sabbath

Read Luke 13:10-17

Find the Missing Word

This woman
was crippled for ___ ___ ⟨○⟩ ___ ___ ___ ___ ___ years.

19

Write About It

What made healing the crippled woman on the Sabbath the right thing for Jesus to do?

Name a time you did the right thing even though it wasn't a popular choice with your friends. Or is there a time you did not do what is right because you were afraid of what your friends would say?

Tiny Treasure

God is faithful in all he does!

Prayer

Lord God, thank you for being faithful. Help me to do the right thing. In Jesus' name, amen.

Do It!

Just as healing on the Sabbath was the right thing for Jesus to do, you too, can show faithfulness to God by doing the right thing for your family, friends, and others who need your help. "Faithful" can be defined as "somebody who or something that can be trusted or depended on." Knowing God is faithful to his children, let's show each other faithfulness by this fun activity.

The Game of TRUST

Object of the Game

Taking turns trusting your family or friends to catch you.

What You Need

- Blindfold

What You Do

One person is blindfolded. The other three people stand behind and to the sides of the blindfolded person. With arms outstretched, the blindfolded person falls backwards trusting their friends or family to catch them. Take turns so that everyone has an opportunity to fall and be caught at least once.

Questions

- How did you feel trusting others would catch you?
- Was it easier being the person depended on to catch?
- When you fell backward, you showed that you trusted the others to catch you. How can you show that you trust God to be faithful to you?
- How can you be faithful to God?

God Forms Families

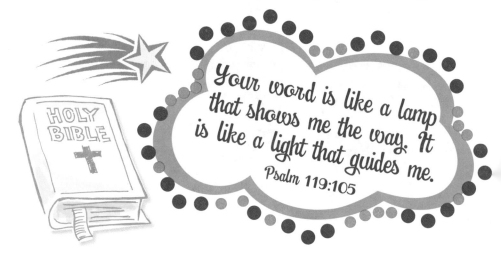

Your word is like a lamp that shows me the way. It is like a light that guides me.

Psalm 119:105

The Valuable Gift

Lauren fingered the brand-new Bible she received from her grandparents for her birthday. She opened the cover and read the words her grandfather wrote,

Dear Lauren,

We hope and pray that the words of this Bible sink deep in your heart. We love you!

Hugs and kisses,

Grandpa and Grandma

Lauren put the Bible down on her dresser, opened the top drawer, and reached in for the white envelope containing money from her family and friends. She wanted to buy a new tablet with that money and she was only ten dollars short. If her grandparents had given her money instead of the Bible, she knew she would have had enough.

"Lauren," Mom called from downstairs. "Telephone. It's your friend Emma."

"I'll be right there." Lauren quickly put the money back in the envelope and shoved it inside her top drawer. She ran down the stairs two at a time and reached out her hand for the phone.

"Slow down, Lauren." Mom laughed.

"Hey, Emma." Lauren turned to go back upstairs to her room.

"So, when do we go to the mall to buy your tablet?" Emma asked.

Lauren sat down on her bed. "It may be a while longer. I'm ten dollars short."

"What do you mean?" Emma asked. "I thought you asked for money from everyone for your birthday this year."

"I did." Lauren glanced over at the Bible sitting on her dresser.

"Well, I guess you'll be doing some extra chores around the house." Emma laughed. "Don't worry, you can make ten dollars in no time."

"Yeah." Lauren sighed into the phone. "I gotta go, see ya."

"Talk to you later," Emma said.

Lauren put the phone down and opened her Bible. She remembered hearing in Sunday school that Psalm 119 was the longest Psalm. As she flipped through the pages, she found Psalm 119 and read verse 105. "Your word is like a lamp that shows me the way. It is like a light that guides me."

Lauren felt a twinge of guilt. How could she have wanted money instead of a Bible from her grandparents? She definitely had outgrown her little kid's Bible, the one her parents gave to her when she was in Kindergarten. She knew all those stories by heart. Maybe it was time for her to grow up a little.

Lauren smiled at the words her grandfather wrote inside the front cover. She loved them, too!

Your Turn

1. Do you enjoy reading the Bible? What is your favorite verse?

2. What does our verse mean when it says that the Bible will guide you?

HOLY BIBLE

96

Bible Story

The Parable of the Sower
Read Matthew 13:1-9;18-23

Find the Missing Word

Seed thrown on ___ ___ ___ ___

___ ___ ___ ◯ produces a crop.
4

Write About It

List all the different types of soil and what happens in each situation from the Parable of the Sower.

97

Describe a time (Sunday school, summer camp, or devotions with your family, etc.) when a Bible verse really helped you get through a situation.

Tiny Treasure

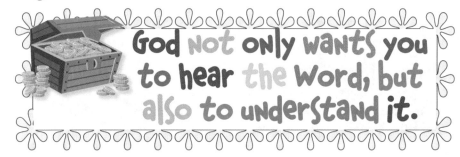

God not only wants you to hear the Word, but also to understand it.

Prayer

Lord God, thank you for the gift of the Bible. Help me to understand how important your Word is for my life. In Jesus' name, amen.

Do It!

Jesus taught by telling stories. You can learn what God wants you to know, too. Try making this fun candle as an example to remind you that God's Word is a lamp and a light.

Beeswax Candle

What You Need

- Sheets of beeswax (approximately 16x8 inches in size)

- Scissors

- Wick

What You Do

1. Fold one sheet of the beeswax in half and press along the fold with your hands to flatten it. Using scissors, cut the sheet of beeswax along the crease.

2. Lay down one of the cut pieces of beeswax. Lay the wick on the edge of the piece of beeswax directly in front of you. At least a half an inch of the piece of wick should extend past each side of the piece of beeswax.

3. Slowly and carefully roll the edge of the beeswax closest to you over the wick. Tuck the edge of the beeswax in around the wick. You want to seal it in so that when you continue rolling your candle it will roll up neatly and evenly.

4. Roll up your candle slowly and carefully with your fingers, pushing the beeswax candle with both hands and applying even pressure. While you are rolling, keep an eye on your edges to roll a nice straight, tight candle.

5. Continue rolling until you are about two inches from the end. Make sure the end of your candle is rolled as tight and even as at the beginning, and that the edges are still straight before you roll up the last of your candle.

6. Seal the edge by rubbing your hands together and using your body heat to warm the wax. Starting in the middle, press your warm fingers gently along the edge of the beeswax. You only need to do this lightly and briefly. You don't want to push down on the edge too hard or you will crush you candle. Continue until the entire edge is molded to the body of the candle.

7. Trim the wick at one end of the candle so it is even with the base. Trim the wick at the other end of the candle to about ¼-inch long.

* Make sure you burn your candle only when a parent is around!

Extra Candle-Making Tips

Experiment with decorating your candles. Heat them slightly with a hair dryer and roll them in glitter, jewels, or flower petals.

God's Delight

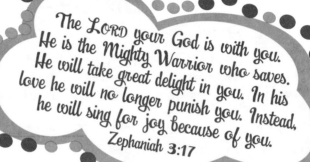

The LORD your God is with you. He is the Mighty Warrior who saves. He will take great delight in you. In his love he will no longer punish you. Instead, he will sing for joy because of you.
Zephaniah 3:17

You Are Special

"Will I ever grow?" Brianna sipped lemonade on the front porch with her dad.

"Of course you will," Dad encouraged.

"All the other kids at school are taller than me." Brianna slurped the last sip of her mom's homemade lemonade. "How come I'm so short anyway?"

'Well, your mom isn't very tall and neither am I."

Brianna picked up a baseball and mitt. "But do you really think I might grow someday?"

Dad reached for the other mitt. "Throw me the ball."

Do you think I will, Dad?" Brianna asked again. She threw a fastball.

You sure got a strong arm." Dad threw the ball back to Brianna.

"Do you think it matters to God whether you are short or tall?"

"Probably not." Brianna tried a curve ball this time.

"I know you don't like being the smallest one in your class." Dad threw the ball back to Brianna. "But there are other things that make you who you are."

"Like my pitching arm." Brianna threw her dad a slider.

"That, and other things," Dad threw a slider of his own.

"How about my good grades in school?" Brianna tossed a knuckle ball too far to the left. She laughed, watching her dad chase the ball down the street.

"I think you need a little work on your knuckle ball." Dad exhaled loudly when he returned. "Yes, your intelligence also makes you special."

Brianna ran to the porch as her mom came out with two more glasses of lemonade. "How about a break, Dad? More lemonade sounds good." She placed her ball and mitt on the small table, accidentally knocking over one of the glasses her mom just poured. "Oops, sorry. I'll run in and get something to clean it up." Brianna came back in a hurry with a handful of paper towels.

"You are also willing to say you're sorry and help when you've made a mistake." Dad helped clean up the spill.

"I may be small," Brianna said. "But I'm closer to the ground when I have to clean things up!"

"Good things come in small packages!" Dad said. "And I love you just the way you are."

Your Turn

1. God loves you just the way you are. What are some things about you that make it easy to believe God loves you? What are some things about you that you think would make it hard for God to love you?

2. Our verse says that God takes great delight in you. How does that make you feel?

Bible Story

The Parables of the
Mustard Seed and the Yeast
Read Matthew 13:31-35

Find the Missing Word

The kingdom of ___ ___ ___ ___ ___ ◯ is like a mustard see

4

Write About It

In the Parable of the Mustard Seed and the Yeast, how does Jesus describe the kingdom of heaven?

Our verse says that God takes great delight in you. How does that make you feel?

Tiny Treasure

God rejoices over you!

Prayer

Lord God, thank you for taking great delight in me! Thank you for loving me just the way I am. In Jesus' name, amen.

Do It!

Jesus takes great joy and pleasure in you. In what ways are you special and unique? Try taking this little quiz to find out!

The Me Quiz

1. If given time to yourself, what would you do?

    a. Read

    b. Play a sport outside

    c. Do arts and crafts

    d. Play an instrument

    e. Make cookies for a sick friend

2. Your teacher asks you to present a book report. What do you do?

    a. Go straight to the library to get started

    b. Find a book about your favorite sports player

    c. Ask your teacher if you can make a picture to go along with your report

    d. Read a book about a musician

    e. Read an autobiography about someone who helped change the world

3. What subject in school do you like the best?

    a. Can't decide—I like them all

    b. RECESS!

    c. Definitely Art

    d. Music

    e. Social Studies

4. What would you like to do to help others?

    a. Be a teacher's helper

    b. Help a coach teach a sport to younger children

    c. Make a get-well card for someone who is sick

    d. Play a musical instrument for people in a nursing home

    e. Take care of a friend's hamster while their family is on vacation

5. What do you want to be when you grow up?

    a. Teacher

    b. Professional Athlete

    c. Artist

    d. Musician

    e. Missionary

Answers:

If you chose mostly:

A, you are the intellectual type. You like most subjects in school and most likely enjoy studying. Congratulations! God made you special.

B, you love the outdoors. You probably play team sports and enjoy winning games. Congratulations! God made you special.

C, you love arts and crafts. You probably have a drawer full of crayons, markers, stickers, and paper. Congratulations! God made you special.

D, you are drawn to music. Maybe you already play a musical instrument or can't wait until you do. Congratulations! God made you special.

E, you enjoy working with your hands. Whether it be cooking or caring for an animal, you just want to serve. Congratulations! God made you special.

God's Faithfulness

> Then you will call out to me.
> You will come and pray
> to me. And I will listen to you.
> Jeremiah 29:12

Saying a Prayer

Emily knelt at the foot of her bed. She'd never tried this before and felt uncomfortable. Normally, she prayed lying down in her bed all snug under the covers. This night, though, she wanted to ask God for something important and she needed to stay awake.

"Dear God," Emily prayed. "Tomorrow is a big day for me. You see, I have my first big piano recital, and I'm scared. What if I forget my song? Or what if I trip on my way to the piano? My dad and stepmom say I'm worrying for nothing, but I'm nervous." Emily laid her head down on her folded hands. "Please, Lord, help me to remember all the notes and play my best. In Jesus' name, amen."

After climbing into bed and turning off her light, Emily shifted to find the most comfortable spot in her bed. She pulled the comforter under her chin and closed her eyes. Before she knew it, the sun peeked its rays into her room.

After climbing out of bed and eating a stack of pancakes, it was time to get ready for the recital. Emily reached into her closet and pulled out the new lavender dress her stepmom, Sandy, bought for this special occasion. Emily fumbled with the buttons, her fingers not

working properly. *Lord, help me to calm down.* As she slipped into her ballet flats, Dad called up the stairs and said it was time to go.

Emily whispered another quick prayer, then grabbed her sheet music. Before getting into the car, she took a deep breath.

"How are you doing?" Sandy asked. "You look a little pale."

"I'll be all right." Emily tightened her grip on her piano book. "I prayed last night that God would help me today."

"You'll do just fine." Dad glanced at her in the rearview mirror.

"Thanks."

When they pulled into the parking lot, Mrs. Emerson waved at them from the front of the church.

Emily let out a nervous giggle. "My piano teacher looks more nervous than me."

Once backstage, Emily peeked out from behind the curtain searching for her parents.

"You're next," Mrs. Emerson said.

"Here goes nothing," Emily muttered to herself. As she walked up to the piano, she saw her parents sitting in the third row on the right-hand side. They smiled at her and nodded their heads as if to say, "You can do it!"

The song flowed from her fingertips, fumbling on only one wrong note. After the recital, her teacher assured her nobody noticed. "You did great," she said as she gave her a one-armed hug and a pink carnation.

That night, Emily once again got on her knees to talk with God. "Thank you for hearing my prayer. I can't wait for my next recital!"

Your Turn

1. Do you have a special prayer you pray at bedtime or other times? Write it down here.

2. Describe a time God answered your prayer. Did God answer in a way you expected or not? Why do you think God answered the way he did?

Bible Story

Jesus Feeds the
Five Thousand
Read Matthew 14:13-21

There were ___ ___ ___ ___ ___ ___ baskets of food left over.

Write About It

What did Jesus do before he fed the five thousand people? Why do you think he did that?

Why do you pray? How does that help you?

Tiny Treasure

God wants a relationship with you.

Prayer

Lord God, thank you that I can come and pray to you. Thank you for always listening to me. In Jesus' name, amen.

Do It!

Just as Jesus prayed before he fed five thousand people, you can pray anytime, too. God will always listen to your prayers. Try making this Prayer Jar not only to write down your prayer requests, but also to see how God answers your prayers.

Prayer Jar

What You Need

- Glass jar, any size

- Tissue paper, different colors

- Glue

- Paintbrush

What You Do

1. Tear the tissue paper into small squares or pieces.

2. Paint a section of the jar with glue.

3. Stick the tissue-paper pieces on the glue.

4. Overlap the tissue-paper pieces, adding glue if needed.

5. Repeat steps 2–4 until the whole jar is covered.

6. Paint a thin layer of glue over the whole jar.

7. Let the jar dry overnight.

8. Write down a prayer request daily on a small piece of paper and put it in the jar. At the end of the week, read the prayer requests and write down how God answered your prayer. If a prayer hasn't been answered yet, put it back in the jar.

God's Strength

Faith is being sure of what we hope for. It is being sure of what we do not see.

Hebrews 11:1

Keep the Faith

Brianna felt as if her friend Hannah was hiding something, but she didn't know what it could be. The past couple of days Brianna had caught Hannah talking with Abigail at recess. Whenever Brianna would walk up to them, the conversation between Hannah and Abigail would stop.

"Hey, you guys," Brianna said. "What's up?"

"What do you mean?" Hannah glanced at Abigail.

"We aren't doing anything." Abigail protested.

"Oh, I didn't mean anything by it." Brianna put her hands deep into her pockets. "I just want to hang out with you two. Is that OK?"

"Of course." Hannah sighed.

When the school bell rang, Brianna was relieved to go back to class.

Once seated in her chair, she quickly scribbled a note to Hannah and reached across the aisle to pass it to her friend. Brianna had to get to the bottom of why Hannah was acting so weird. If Hannah checked the "yes" box, it meant she would tell Brianna what was going on at lunch. But if she checked "no," it meant she wouldn't tell

her. Hannah had been her best friend for years. Brianna was certain Hannah would check "yes" and tell her the big secret.

When Hannah reached across the aisle to pass the note back, Brianna's hands grew clammy and her stomach felt strange. When she opened the note, she couldn't believe her eyes! Hannah had checked the box marked "no"!

For the next two hours until the lunch bell rang, Brianna tried to concentrate on math and science, but it was nearly impossible. She searched the cafeteria to sit by her sister. Elizabeth gave Brianna a funny look as she placed her lunch on the table and sat down.

"What are you doing?" Elizabeth asked.

"Joining you for lunch." Brianna dug into her brown paper sack for her tuna fish sandwich.

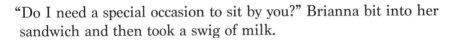

"Why?" Elizabeth asked. "You never sit by me at lunch.
What's the special occasion?"

"Do I need a special occasion to sit by you?" Brianna bit into her sandwich and then took a swig of milk.

"All right," Elizabeth said. "What's up?"

"That's funny," Brianna said. "I asked my friends that same question last recess and they ignored me."

"Friend trouble, huh?" Elizabeth asked. "So, you want to intrude on me and my friends to make yourself feel better."

"Never mind." Brianna stood to leave.
"I'll get out of your way. Pretend I never sat here."

"OK," Elizabeth said. "See you after school."

Brianna hung her head as she headed toward the garbage can to throw away the rest of her lunch. *God, I know you are always there for me even though I can't see you,* Brianna prayed silently.

Without looking where she was going, she nearly ran into Hannah.

"Brianna," Hannah said. "Where have you been?"

"Trying to eat lunch with Elizabeth."

"Why?" Hannah gave Brianna a funny look.

Because I was trying to stay away from you! Brianna thought, but didn't say. Instead, she blurted out angrily, "So, what is the big secret, anyway?"

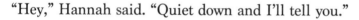

"Hey," Hannah said. "Quiet down and I'll tell you."

"If you really want to." Brianna placed her hands on her hips.

"I didn't want to hurt you," Hannah said, "but I guess I already have."

"And . . ."

"Abigail invited me to a sleepover this weekend." Hannah continued. "I didn't want you to find out, so I've been trying to talk with her when you're not around. I'm sorry."

"So that's the big secret?" Brianna asked. "That's no big deal. I'm just glad you're still my best friend."

"Always!" Hannah said.

Brianna smiled. "Thanks."

Your Turn

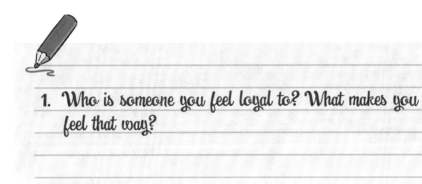

1. Who is someone you feel loyal to? What makes you feel that way?

2. Our verse says that faith in God will give you strength. How can God's strength help you when you're having friend trouble? How can it help you stay loyal?

Bible Story

Jesus Walks on Water

Read Matthew 14:22-36

Find the Missing Word

The disciples thought Jesus was a 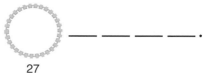 —— —— —— ——.

27

Write About It

How do you think the story would have gone if Peter had kept his eyes on Jesus when he was walking on the water?

118

How do you think your life will be different if you keep your eyes on God?

Tiny Treasure

God will make you strong when you keep your eyes on him.

Prayer

Lord God, thank you for giving me strength when I keep my eyes on you. I know you are there even though I can't see you. In Jesus' name, amen.

Do It!

Just as Peter needed to keep his eyes on Jesus, you too, can keep the faith when things get tough. God is always there for you even though you can't see him. Try this fun activity to illustrate faith that something is there even when you can't see it.

Rice Game

Object of the Game

Find as many safety pins as you can in a given amount of time. For two or more players.

What You Need

- A bowl
- Uncooked rice (about 4 cups)
- Small gold safety pins (at least 20)
- Blindfold
- Stopwatch or watch with second hand

What You Do

1. Pour the uncooked rice in a bowl.

2. Mix in the safety pins. Make sure they're closed!

3. Blindfold one of the players and have them try to remove as many safety pins as they can in one minute.

The rice and safety pins feel very similar, so you may end up with a pile of rice! Now try removing the safety pins without the blindfold. Too easy? How much easier our life would be if we kept our eyes on Jesus!

God Makes Each Day

> The LORD has done it on this day. Let us be joyful today and be glad.
>
> Psalm 118:24

History

98.6

The New Day

The alarm clock went off at 7 A.M. Savannah moaned and rolled over, covering her head with the blankets. Why did she wake up some mornings grouchy at the world?

Savannah knew why she was grumpy this morning. She had a history test and she didn't study. Last night, she was talking on the phone with her soccer friend Jessica and she lost track of time. When she finally hung up, she had to get ready for bed.

Maybe she could pretend to be sick. That way, her teacher would let her make up the test and she could spend part of the day studying.

"Savannah, time to get ready for school," Mom said, peeking her head in Savannah's bedroom.

"I don't feel so good." Savannah couldn't look at her mom.

"What hurts?" Concern was in Mom's voice.

"My stomach," Savannah said. "I think I have the flu."

"Let me check your temperature," Mom said. "I'll be right back with the thermometer."

A few moments later, as Savannah lay there with the thermometer under her tongue, her stomach growled.

Mom looked at her. "Well, sounds like someone is hungry.

She pulled the thermometer out and looked at it. "Ninety-eight point six degrees. Normal."

"OK," Savannah said, sitting up in bed. "I feel fine. What's for breakfast?"

"Why did you pretend to be sick?" Mom gave her a questioning look. "What's going on in school today?"

Savannah sat there wondering what to say. If she told her mom the truth, she might get in trouble. But if she didn't tell the truth, her mom would probably find out anyway.

"Are you going to tell me? I know you're hungry for breakfast, and the sooner you tell me, the sooner you'll eat."

Savannah took a big breath. "I didn't want to go to school because I didn't study for my history test. If I take the test today, I will get a bad grade."

"I see," Mom said. "So, you thought if you stayed home today, you could take the test another day?"

"Yes," Savannah said, hopeful her mom would agree.

"Sorry, Savannah, but you need to go to school today and take your history test." Mom stood and headed for the door.

"I thought you'd say that." Savannah swung her legs off the edge of the bed. "I'll be downstairs in a few minutes."

Before going to the kitchen for breakfast, Savannah checked her computer. A note from Jessica was in her inbox.

Hey, friend! What a beautiful day! Aren't you glad God made today?

Love, Jessica

Savannah ate her pancakes with a smile. No matter what grade she got on her history test, Savannah was glad for the day God made. And next time, she'll talk less and study more.

Your Turn

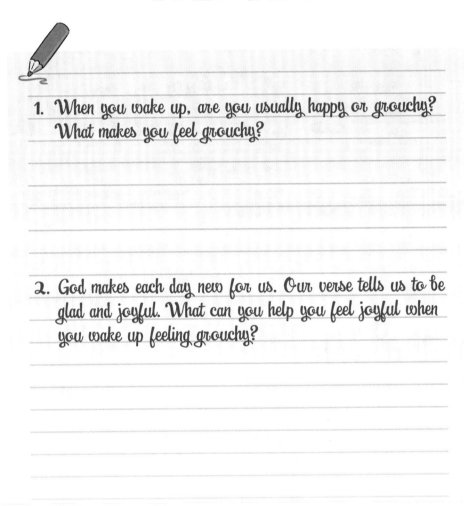

1. When you wake up, are you usually happy or grouchy? What makes you feel grouchy?

2. God makes each day new for us. Our verse tells us to be glad and joyful. What can you help you feel joyful when you wake up feeling grouchy?

Bible Story

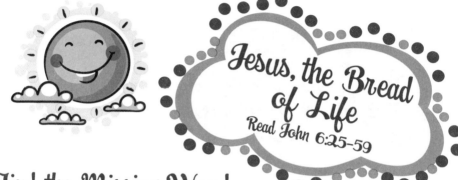

Jesus, the Bread of Life
Read John 6:25-59

Find the Missing Word

Jesus is the ___ ⭕ ___ ___ ___ that came down from heaven.

9

Write About It

How can you explain to your friends that Jesus is the Bread of Life? (Verse 35 is the key.) Write down verse 35 in your own words.

How will knowing Jesus is the Bread of Life help you rejoice for today and every day?

Tiny Treasure

God wants you to be glad for each day.

Prayer

Lord God, thank you for this day you made. Help me to rejoice for each day. In Jesus' name, amen.

Do It!

Just as Jesus taught that whomever feeds on the Bread of Life will live forever, you too can live forever in heaven if you believe on him. Try baking this bread recipe to remind you that Jesus is the Bread of Life and to enjoy each day that God has made.

Bread in a Bag

What You Need

- 3 cups all-purpose flour, divided

- 3 tablespoons white sugar

- 1 (.25 ounce) package rapid rise yeast

- 1 cup warm water

- 3 tablespoons non-fat dry milk

- 3 tablespoons olive oil

- 1½ teaspoons salt

What You Do

1. Preheat the oven to 375°F.

2. In a large resealable freezer bag, combine 1 cup of flour with the sugar, yeast, and warm water. Squeeze most of the air out of the bag, and seal.

3. Squish the contents of the bag with your hands until well blended. Set aside to rest for 10 minutes at room temperature, or until bubbles appear.

4. In a separate bowl, stir together 1 cup of flour, the dry milk, oil, and salt. Pour into the resealable bag, squeeze out most of the air, and seal.

5. Squish the contents until well blended. Add the last cup of flour to the bag, and continue squishing until well blended.

6. Remove the dough from the resealable bag, and place on a floured surface. Knead dough for five to eight minutes.

7. Form dough into a small loaf, and place in a greased 8x4-inch loaf pan. Cover with a towel, and allow to rise for about 30 minutes, or until your finger leaves an impression when you poke the top of the loaf gently.

8. Bake the bread for 35 minutes, or until golden brown. Remove from oven and set aside to cool completely.

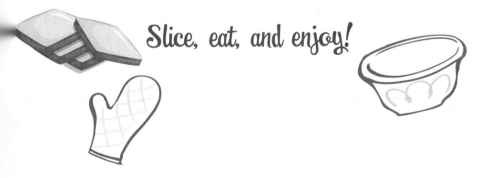

Slice, eat, and enjoy!

★ WEEK-10

God Saves

> Say with your mouth, "Jesus is Lord." Believe in your heart that God raised him from the dead. Then you will be saved.
> Romans 10:9

I Will See Him Again

Tears flowed from Lauren's eyes. Grandma had called and told her family that Grandpa had died in his sleep. It couldn't be true! How would she live without her favorite grandpa? Lauren reached for the Bible her grandparents had given her and touched the words her grandpa wrote for her in the front. Lauren knew one day she would see her grandpa again in heaven, but it didn't make the pain any less today.

"Lauren," Mom called. "Can you come here, please?"

"Coming." Lauren wiped her eyes and headed downstairs.

Mom hugged Lauren tight. "Are you OK?"

"I guess," Lauren said. "I know Grandpa was old, but it still hurts."

"He lived a great life," Mom said.

"I wish he lived to be at least one hundred years old." Lauren slouched down on the couch. "Grandma will be so lonely without him."

"We all will." Mom sat beside her. "He was a great Christian man."

"Can you tell me a story about Grandpa?" Lauren asked, needing some comfort.

"There was a time when I was a little girl that I will never forget," Mom said.

"Go on," Lauren edged closer, eager to listen.

"Well, your grandpa worked as a business man in a big office. One day, the president of the company had to let many of the workers go because business was slow. He couldn't afford to pay them anymore. So, your grandpa and many of his office friends were out of a job. They packed up their belongings and left the building."

"Then what happened?" Lauren hugged a pillow to her chest.

"Your grandma, my mom, received a phone call from Grandpa that night. He said to make lot of beef stew, along with her delicious cornbread and pie for dessert because they were going to have many people over for dinner."

Lauren shook her head in disbelief. "Why would he do that when he just lost his job?"

"That's the great part," Mom said, smiling. "Your grandpa knew he may never see some of those people again, and he wanted to make sure he shared the Bible and what Jesus did on the cross so that one day he may see them in heaven."

"How did he do that?" Lauren asked.

"When everyone arrived at our house and sat down for dinner, he picked up his Bible, opened it and began to read. As a child, I was amazed that my dad's first priority was telling his coworkers about Jesus."

"Wow," Lauren said. "Did anyone decide to follow Jesus that night?"

"Three," Mom said. "And I'm sure Grandpa is finding out if there were others right now in heaven."

"I'm glad I will see Grandpa again," Lauren said. "Because I'm sure going to miss him here on earth."

Your Turn

1. What do you think heaven is like? Who do you want to see there?

2. Have you decided to follow Jesus? If not, what is stopping you?

Bible Story

Zaccaeus
Read Luke 19:1-10

Find the Missing Word

Zacchaeus climbed a ___ ◯ ___ ___ to see Jesus.

12

Write About It

What was Zacchaeus's job? What did Zacchaeus say in verse 8 to show he had a change of heart?

Ask a friend or family member to tell you about the time they decided to follow Jesus. Write about it here.

Tiny Treasure

God wants his children to be saved.

Prayer

Lord God, thank you for sending Jesus to Earth so that I can become a member of your family and spend eternity with you. In Jesus' name, amen.

Do It!

Just as Jesus went to Zacchaeus's house to seek and to save what was lost, you too, can help save the lost by sharing salvation with others. Try this fun activity as a reminder to tell others about Jesus so that you can plant seeds for salvation.

Planting Marigolds

Decorate your own clay flowerpot and plant a marigold, which is also known as calendula. Marigold is an easy plant to grow that is edible and grows quickly. It blooms midsummer until the frost in the fall and is perfect for a first plant.

What You Need

- Marigold seeds
- Potting soil
- 8- to 10-inch clay pot
- 1-inch foam brush
- Fine-point paintbrush
- White paint
- Variety of colored craft paints

What You Do

Painting the Pot

1. Brush a coat of primer paint on the surface of the clay pot. Let it dry. You may paint the top of the pot a different color or use dots, stripes, zig zags, etc. to decorate.

2. Let each color dry before adding another. Allow the pot to dry completely for a day or so before using.

Planting the Seeds

3. Place small rocks in the bottom of the pot for drainage, and fill with potting soil about an inch from the top.

4. Place four seeds in the soil, poking them in lightly. They should be evenly spaced so there is an equal amount of room between each one and the edge of the pot. (If all four come up you will have to thin them later by choosing two of the best-looking seedlings.)

5. Cover the seeds with more soil until the pot is almost filled. Water lightly, making sure the soil is moistened, but the seeds are not disturbed.

6. Place the pot in a sunny spot outside on a deck, porch, or on a windowsill. Be sure you do not let the soil dry out. Instead, keep the soil moist until the seedlings appear.

7. When the plant grows larger and is well established, watering once a day will be fine. On very hot days it may need to be watered twice if it's kept outside.

8. Pinch off the blooms as they wither, and more will continue to grow. Near the end of the summer, stop pinching the flowers off, and seeds will form. You can dry and harvest your seeds by letting them dry on the plant. You can also collect and save the seeds for next year.

God Our King

> Sing the praises of the LORD. He rules from his throne in Zion. Tell among the nations what he has done.
> Psalm 9:11

Who's Your Hero?

"Hey, Hannah, are you going to watch *Adventures of Kaloni* tonight?" Brianna asked during the first recess at school. "She's the best action hero on TV!"

"I sure am," Hannah said. "I just hope I get all my homework done before the show starts."

"Me, too." Brianna practiced some karate moves she learned from her favorite star.

"I like the way she always catches the bad guys," Hannah said.

"Yeah." Brianna nodded her head. "And without anyone knowing she's the hero."

The bell rang, interrupting their conversation.

The afternoon dragged on and on as Brianna's anticipation to watch the show grew. She daydreamed through three classes about how Kaloni was going to save the world.

"Brianna." Her teacher stood by her desk. "Pay attention to your work. What has you so pre-occupied?"

Caught off-guard, Brianna scrambled to find an answer.

She couldn't think fast enough.

"You are such a great student, but I've noticed Tuesdays are difficult for you to concentrate."

"Well . . . my favorite TV show is on tonight," Brianna blurted before thinking of anything else to say.

"Let's concentrate on your work so you will be able to watch it," her teacher said.

Seeing the firm look on her teacher's face pushed Brianna to get back to work. What Mrs. Smith said was true. If she didn't finish her homework, she wouldn't be able to watch her new favorite show. And she'd do anything to make sure she didn't miss it!

Brianna thought about the time she missed a church activity to watch the show. The leaders talked to the kids for months about the importance of the service project they would do together. Brianna looked forward to learning how to share her faith with others, but somehow, when the show's first episode was on the same night, she chose TV over church. Her parents forgot, so Brianna just didn't mention it.

She had a hard time fully enjoying the show that night. If she could do it all over again, she'd go on the youth group outing. It not only would please her parents, but more importantly, it would keep God number one in her life.

The school bell rang. Brianna sighed at the homework she would need to take home.

"See you tomorrow," Hannah said.

"Bye." Brianna gathered her books and put them in her backpack. "We'll talk all about Kaloni tomorrow at recess."

Hannah gave her the thumbs-up sign as she ran out of the school doors.

Brianna smiled to herself. Only five more hours until the next episode.

Your Turn

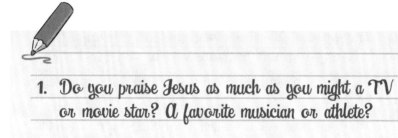

1. Do you praise Jesus as much as you might a TV or movie star? A favorite musician or athlete?

2. How can you show that Jesus is your King?

Bible Story

The Triumphal Entry
Read John 12:12-19

Find the Missing Word

They took palm —— —— —— —— —— ——

and went out to meet Jesus.

28

Write About It

Tell about a time you put something or someone else before God.
How did that make you feel later?

What are ways you can put God number one in your life?

Tiny Treasure

God wants you to praise him for what he has done.

Prayer

Lord God, thank you for being my King and for what your Son has done for me. Help me to keep you number one in my life. In Jesus' name, amen.

Do It!

Just as Jesus' triumphal entry into Jerusalem brought praise from the crowd, you too, can praise Jesus by keeping him number one in your life. Think about what God has done in your life throughout the day and thank him before you go to sleep at night.

 Listening to Christian music is a great way to praise and worship God. Ask your parents to turn their car radios to your local Christian station. Sing along!

Here's a way you can introduce your friends to your favorite Christian artists. Choose a favorite Christian song. Make a poster of the lyrics and give it to a friend.

Song Poster

What You Need

- Markers or paint pens

- Sheet of poster board

Optional

- Stickers or adhesive-back craft-foam shapes, especially musical shapes.

What You Do

1. Use markers or paint pens to copy the words of the song you've chosen.

2. Add additional drawings or decorations. Optional: Add stickers or adhesive-back craft-foam shapes.

3. When you give the poster to your friend, consider giving them a CD with the song on it.

God's Child

Some people did accept him and did believe in his name. He gave them the right to become children of God.

John 1:12

Accepting Jesus

"Savannah," Dad called. "Your ride is here."

Every Sunday for the past month, Savannah was able to go to church with her friend Jessica and her family. Savannah really enjoyed going to church to find out more about the Bible.

"Here I come." She raced to the front door. "Bye, Mom. Bye, Dad. See you later."

Savannah hopped into the back-passenger seat next to Jessica and her little brother, Tyler.

"Hey," Jessica said. "I'm glad you could come today."

"Me, too." Savannah folded her hands in her lap. She glanced over at the Bible on Jessica's lap and suddenly her hands felt empty. Oh, how she wished she had a Bible. That way, she could read it all week and know more about the Bible stories they talked about on Sunday mornings.

"Here we are." Jessica's dad pulled into the church parking lot. Jessica grabbed Savannah's arm and they took off in a sprint to their Sunday-school room.

Once seated, the Sunday-school teacher introduced a special speaker, Ms. Harper, a missionary. Ms. Harper not only talked about Africa, but also had a slideshow to show them pictures. Ms. Harper was a nurse, and she helped the many children who had illnesses or diseases.

Ms. Harper said, "I want to tell you something very important that I tell the children in Africa. Do you know that God loves you? He loves you so much! First John 3:1 says we are called children of God!"

Savannah felt butterflies in her stomach as the missionary talked on about how to become a member of God's family. She knew that it was the right time for her to have a personal relationship with Jesus. When Sunday school was nearly over, Savannah shyly approached Ms. Harper. "I want to follow Jesus and become a member of God's family," Savannah said, her voice timid.

"Wonderful," Ms. Harper said. "Do you believe that God sent his Son Jesus to Earth to die for your sins?" Ms. Harper asked.

"Yes." Savannah nodded her head.

"Do you believe God resurrected Jesus from the dead and that he now sits on the right hand of God?" Ms. Harper asked. Savannah nodded again. "Will you pray with me to accept Jesus as Lord of your life?" Ms. Harper asked. Savannah bowed her head and folded her hands.

 "Just repeat after me," Ms. Harper said. "Dear Father in heaven, I come to you in the name of Jesus. I am a sinner, and I am very sorry for my sins. I need your forgiveness. I believe that Jesus Christ died on the cross and shed his blood for my sins. You said in the Bible, that if we say that Jesus is Lord and believe in our hearts that God raised Jesus from the dead, we would be saved (Romans 10:9). Right now, I say that Jesus is Lord. I accept Jesus Christ as my own personal Savior.

"Thank you, Jesus for dying for me and giving me eternal life. Amen." After the prayer, Ms. Harper gave Savannah a big hug. "You are now a child of the King!"

"Thank you!" Savannah said, hugging back.

"Every one of God's children needs one of these." Ms. Harper reached into a brown box and handed Savannah a brand-new Bible.

"My very own Bible," she whispered in awe. "Thank you!"

Savannah returned to Jessica. "Now I know what I want to do when I'm older. I'm going to be a nurse in Africa!"

Your Turn

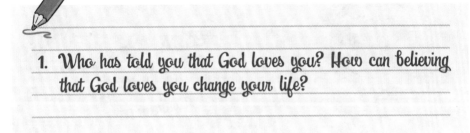

1. Who has told you that God loves you? How can believing that God loves you change your life?

2. If you have decided to follow Jesus and make him the Lord of your life, what do you remember about the day you made the decision?

Bible Story

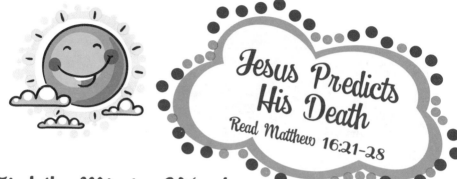

Jesus Predicts
His Death
Read Matthew 16:21-28

Find the Missing Word

To follow Christ, you must deny yourself, take up his

___ ___ ___ ___ ( ) and follow him.

16

Write About It

How do you think Jesus' disciples felt when Jesus predicted his own death?

Can you list some of the spiritual blessings we have as God's children? (See Ephesians 1:3–14)

Tiny Treasure

God gave you the right to be called his child.

Prayer

Lord God, thank you for allowing me to be your child. In Jesus' name, amen.

Do It!

Just as Jesus explained to the disciples what they must do to follow him, you too, can follow Christ and become his child. Link your heart to Jesus with this fun craft.

String of Hearts

What You Need

- Construction paper
- Ruler
- Pencil
- Scissors
- Markers

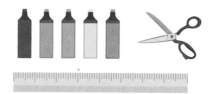

What You Do

1. Cut out two strips of paper 2½ inches wide and 9 inches long. (Construction paper is 9 inches wide.)
2. Tape the two strips together to form one strip of paper 2½ inches wide and 18 inches long.
3. Fold the strip accordion style in sections 2½ inches wide.
4. On the top layer, draw a heart. Make sure the sides of the heart extend out to the folded edges.
5. Cut through all the layers of paper except where the sides of the heart touch the paper folds.
6. In the middle of your heart chain, print each letter of "Jesus" on a separate heart.

Optional: Use markers to add more decorations to hearts.

Put your String of Hearts up in your bedroom as a reminder to link your heart to Jesus.

God's Kindness

Family Ties

> LORD, you are forgiving and good. You are full of love for all who call out to you.
>
> Psalm 86:5

Swish! Lauren made a basket. She dribbled for a lay-up. *Bounce, bounce*, and *swish!* Lauren was just about to throw a free throw when Aunt Janet's car pulled up to the curb. "Hi, Lauren," Aunt Janet called as she stepped out of the car.

"Hi, Aunt Janet. Hi, Ryan." Lauren's voice dropped a notch.

She and her cousin Ryan had their ups and downs. They either got along great or drove each other crazy. They were just too different, she had concluded after one visit. *Good thing we don't see each other much*, she thought.

"Hi, Lauren." Ryan pushed up his glasses and shut the car door.

"I'm going inside to talk with your mom," Aunt Janet said.

"Sure you don't want to play some hoops?" Lauren asked.

"No thanks," Aunt Janet said. "Maybe Ryan would like to."

Lauren noticed the look Ryan gave his mom. He never did like to play sports. He would rather spend his time building model airplanes or reading the encyclopedia.

"OK, I'll play," Ryan said.

149

"Really?" Lauren twirled the ball on one finger like her dad had taught her.

"Unless you'd rather do something else?" Ryan asked.

"How about we play P-I-G." Lauren knew the game would end in five minutes.

"All right." Ryan caught the ball Lauren threw to him. He tossed the ball granny style toward the hoop and missed by at least five feet.

"My turn." Lauren tried not to laugh. She threw the ball from the side edge of the driveway. *Swish!* "You got to make it from here." Lauren pointed to where she had stood.

"Can we just say you won?" Ryan sounded defeated.

"Give up already?" Lauren grinned. "OK, I'll go get us something to drink. I'll be right back."

Lauren didn't mean to eavesdrop, but as she entered the kitchen from the side door, she heard her aunt talking to her mom in the family room.

"I feel so bad for him," Aunt Janet said. "His best friend moved away last weekend. Ryan is so shy and quiet. It took him years to find a friend that understood his intelligence and sensitive nature. He's been so sad lately."

"I'm sure Lauren is helping him feel better," Mom said.

Lauren quietly opened the refrigerator, grabbed two sodas, and quickly headed back outside. She thought about how she'd been so busy showing off her basketball skills that she hadn't paid attention to how Ryan was feeling.

"Here's your soda," Lauren said to her cousin. "Why don't we sit down on the grass?" They sat down. "So, what's new with you?" Lauren said. "Blow up any chemicals lately in your basement lab?"

"Ha ha." Ryan said sarcastically. He took a few gulps of his soda and burped out loud. "Good one!" laughed Lauren.

"Can I tell you something?" Ryan turned a slight shade of pink. "My best friend moved away. I've been really sad. I have no other friends, and I don't think I ever will."

"Don't say that," Lauren said. "I'm sure someone else will be your friend." After a few minutes of silence, she added, "I'll be your friend!"

"You're my cousin." Ryan pushed up his glasses.

"Yeah," Lauren said. "But we can be friends too, right?" She extended her hand for a handshake.

"Right." Ryan shook it firmly. "Friends. Thanks."

"How about another game of P-I-G?" Lauren tossed her empty soda can into the recycling bin in the garage.

"No way!" Ryan gave Lauren a little shove.

Your Turn

1. Our verse says that God is kind and forgiving. Does knowing this make a difference in the way you treat your family and friends? Even if your family or friends are different than you?

2. What can be harder if your family and friends are different than you? What can you do to make it less difficult to be kind and forgiving of people who are different than you?

Bible Story

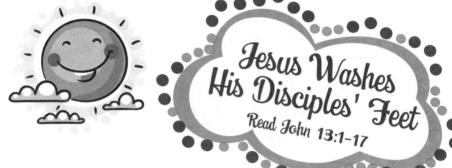

Jesus Washes His Disciples' Feet

Read John 13:1–17

Find the Missing Word

Jesus dried the disciples' feet with a ——— ——— ——— ◯ ———.

17

Write About It

Why did Jesus wash his disciples' feet?

Can you give an example of kindness that you showed to someone?

Tiny Treasure

God has so much love for you!

Prayer

Lord God, thank you for your kindness. Help us to be kind to others. In Jesus' name, amen.

Do It!

Jesus gave an example of kindness by washing the disciples' feet. You can follow Jesus' example and show kindness to others. Pick one or all of these acts of kindness. It will put a smile on YOUR face.

You could also give yourself a "Kindness Score." Each day for a month, count up the number of things you did on this list. Give yourself a point for each thing. You can also earn extra points by showing acts of kindness not included in the list!

Twenty Ways to Show Kindness:

- Give family and friends "kindness coupons" they can cash-in for special favors.

- Offer to help your neighbor do some yard work.

- Write notes to or bring flowers or goodies to your teachers and others at your school who don't normally receive any recognition, like the cleaning people or office staff.

- With parent permission, send someone you know an animated greeting card on the Internet.

- Leave a muffin or a handmade note of thanks for your mail-delivery person.

- Tell your dad or mom that you think they do a great job.

- Remind a friend or family member that they are very important in your life.

- Write a note to a friend or someone who has helped you, praising them for who they are.

- Make a friend laugh when they are feeling sad.

- Do the dishes even though it's not your turn.

- Buy a box of popsicles to share with neighbor kids on a hot day.

  - Give a compliment.

  - Clean your room and surprise your parents.

- Go through your photos, and send a picture to a friend.

- Give books in good condition to your local library or school during a book drive.

- Tell someone you love and appreciate them.

  - Play nicely with your sibling(s).

  - If you make a mistake, say "I'm sorry."

Sorry! - Offer to take the dog for a walk.

- Say "please" and "thank you."

God Can Be Trusted

> Trust in the LORD with all your heart.
> Do not depend on your own understanding.
> In all your ways obey him. Then he will make
> your paths smooth and straight.
> Proverbs 3:5-6

Tea for Two

"Let's start with 'Concerto in C Minor,'" Emily's piano teacher, Mrs. Emerson, said one Tuesday afternoon.

Emily put her fingers on the piano keys. As she began to play, she fumbled three times before starting on the right notes. "I'm just a little distracted." Emily wiggled her fingers to loosen them up.

"Do you want to talk about it?"

Emily stared at the piano keys. "I do need to talk to someone."

"This calls for some tea and cookies." Mrs. Emerson smiled.

"Sure." Emily followed her piano teacher into the kitchen.

"Why don't you sit at the kitchen table while I get everything ready," Mrs. Emerson said.

Emily watched her teacher put water on to boil and then open the cabinets. She reached up and took out the prettiest tea set Emily had ever seen. "Would you rather have the cup with the lavender flowers or the pink ones?" Mrs. Emerson asked.

"Pink," replied Emily, smiling.

Mrs. Emerson placed four shortbread cookies on a green leaf-shaped plate and set it down in the middle of the table. After pouring the tea,

Mrs. Emerson carried the steaming teacups to the table. "What seems to be troubling you?" Mrs. Emerson said, getting right to the point.

Emily grabbed a cookie and dunked it into her tea. "My stepmom's going to have a baby," she said, and then quickly took a bite of the now soggy cookie.

"That's wonderful news, isn't it?" Mrs. Emerson asked.

"Not for me!" Emily leaned back in her chair. "The problem is that this baby will be my dad and my stepmom's child. I'm the one who's going to be left out."

"I know your parents pretty well, and I don't think they would do that." Mrs. Emerson picked up the leaf plate and offered Emily another cookie. "Can I read something to you?" Mrs. Emerson said, opening the drawer to a china cabinet sitting next to the kitchen table.

Emily noticed the book Mrs. Emerson grabbed was a Bible. "All right," she said.

Mrs. Emerson opened the Bible where a bookmark marked the page. "John 14:1 says, 'Do not let your hearts be troubled. You believe in God. Believe in me also.' There are also many other verses about trust. Proverbs 3:5–6 is a great Scripture to memorize."

Sipping the last of her tea, Emily realized she had to not only trust her dad and stepmom with the coming of this new baby, but also trust that God would take care of her.

"How about we play a duet together on the piano?" Mrs. Emerson said.

"Sounds great," Emily said, as she stood to her feet. "Thanks for the tea and cookies. And the talk." She carefully carried her cup and saucer to the sink.

"Anytime," Mrs. Emerson said. "We'll do it again soon."

"Cool," Emily said, leading her teacher back to the piano.

Your Turn

1. How can you show that you trust your family and friends? When might it be hard to trust them?

2. Why do you think that God can be trusted? If you don't trust God, why not?

Bible Story

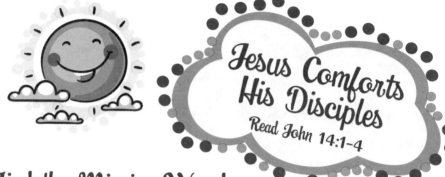

Jesus Comforts
His Disciples
Read John 14:1-4

Find the Missing Word

There are many ___ ___ ___ ◯ ___ in your Father's house.

14

Write About It

What did Jesus say he would be doing for the disciples in John 14:1–4?

When are times you might need comforting? How can trusting in Jesus comfort you?

Tiny Treasure

God wants us to trust him with all our hearts.

Prayer

Lord God, thank you that I can trust in you. Help me to acknowledge you so that you will make my paths smooth and straight. In Jesus' name, amen.

Do It!

Jesus taught his disciples to trust in him, and you can trust Jesus to take care of you, too. "In God We Trust" is written on our money. Try playing this money game to remind you to trust God—not money—to take care of your needs.

In God We Trust Money Game

What You Need

- 10 pennies

- 10 nickels

- 10 dimes

- 10 quarters

Figure out the equal number of pennies, nickels, dimes and/or quarters you will need to match the total in each scenario.

1. The cookie jar was full of coins. There were an equal number of nickels, dimes, and quarters. The total was $3.60. How many are there of each?

Nickels	
Dimes	
Quarters	

2. My friend was scrounging around for loose change in his mom's car floorboard. There were an equal number of pennies, dimes, and quarters. The total was $1.08. How many are there of each?

Pennies	
Dimes	
Quarters	

3. Mom was cleaning out her purse and found lots of change. There were an equal number of nickels, dimes, and quarters. The total was $4.00. How many are there of each?

Nickels	
Dimes	
Quarters	

4. Dad found some loose change in his pocket. There were an equal number of pennies, nickels, and quarters. The total was $2.17. How many are there of each?

Pennies	
Nickels	
Quarters	

5. You counted the change from your piggy bank. There were an equal number of pennies, nickels, and quarters. The total was $2.79. How many are there of each?

Pennies	
Nickels	
Quarters	

6. Your sister found some change on the sidewalk. There were an equal number of pennies, nickels, and quarters. The total was $1.24. How many are there of each?

Pennies	
Nickels	
Quarters	

7. You asked your dad for some change to buy lunch in the cafeteria. Your dad gave you an equal number of nickels, dimes, and quarters. The total was $3.20. How many are there of each?

Nickels	
Dimes	
Quarters	

*Answers found on page 220.

God of Joy

> Sing joyfully to God! He gives us strength. Give a loud shout to the God of Jacob!
> Psalm 81:1

A Day to Rejoice

Adoption Day was finally here! Jessica jumped out of bed and ran into her little brother's bedroom. "Tyler, Tyler. Hey, sleepyhead, do you know what day it is?" She gently shook her two-year-old brother's shoulder.

Tyler's eyes fluttered open, but he closed them once again.

"Hey, you! Wake up! Today is a big day!" Jessica said. "We're going to see the judge and adopt you!"

Tyler stretched and rubbed his eyes.

"Mom wants you to wear that little suit hanging on the doorknob."

He took one look at the three-piece suit and smiled. "Look like Daddy." He hopped down from his bed.

Jessica stopped him with a hand. "I think Mom wants you to eat breakfast before you put it on."

Dad came into the room. "You two are up early."

"It's Adoption Day, so of course we're up early!" Jessica swung her arms in a dramatic fashion. "I've waited a long time for this day. He's officially going to be my brother!" She picked Tyler up, hugged him tight, and twirled him around.

"I'm glad you are so happy," Dad said, laughing. "But you'd better put him down before he gets sick on your nightgown."

Jessica gently sat him on his bed. "What's for breakfast, Dad?"

"I think Mom is making scrambled eggs and bacon. Why don't we go downstairs to find out?"

Jessica skipped down the stairs two at a time while Dad carried Tyler.

"You sure have a lot of energy today." Mom set the table. "Why don't you help me while I tend to the eggs?"

"Is nobody else excited?" Jessica made sure each plate had a fork and spoon.

"Of course we are." Mom smiled. "We've waited for this day for almost two years!"

After breakfast, Mom helped Tyler get into his new blue suit complete with bow tie. Jessica wore a pretty pink top with her blue denim skirt. Mom and Dad dressed like they were going to church.

The courthouse was five blocks away. After going through security, they met with the social worker and were escorted to the judge's chambers. Mom and Dad signed some papers and then the judge said a few words.

"I love days like this when I can join a family together." Judge Barton stood behind his desk. "Will you promise to take care of Tyler—physically, mentally, emotionally, and spiritually? Will you promise to love him and take care of him as your son?"

Mom and Dad smiled at each other and said, "We do."

"He is now Tyler Grant!" Judge Barton smiled and signed the papers.

"I wish we could do that all over again," Jessica said as they made their way to the car. She made everyone laugh.

"God is so good!" Mom turned to look in the back seat where Jessica and her new brother now sat. "Let's go celebrate!"

Your Turn

1. What makes you happy or joyful? Our verse says to sing with joy. What are some other ways to show you feel joyful?

2. How can you get strength from God? Which of God's promises give you strength?

Bible Story

The Parable of the Lost Coin
Read Luke 15:8-10

Find the Missing Word

A woman had ten ⬭ ____ ____ ____ coins.

25

Write About It

Why did the woman in the Parable of the Lost Coin call her friends and neighbors together when she found the missing coin?

Tell about a time when you rejoiced over a situation. It could be a time when you found something that was lost, or it could be another happy occasion.

Tiny Treasure

God wants you to sing for joy!

Prayer

Lord God, thank you so much for bringing joy to my life. Help me to find something to be joyful about during the difficult days. In Jesus' name, amen.

Do It!

Just as the woman rejoiced when she found her lost coin, you too, can find something to rejoice about in your life. JOY is a tiny word that can have so much impact on those around us. We can share joy with others by giving family and friends these colorful bookmarks.

Joy Bookmarks

What You Need

- Construction paper or poster board

- Ruler

- Scissors

- Markers, colored pencils, or watercolors and brushes

- Decorative materials: stickers, photos, glue, glitter, adhesive-backed craft-foam shapes, or rubber stamps and stamp pads

- Clear Con-Tact paper

- Hole punch

- Ribbon

Optional

- Pinking shears or other decorative-edge scissors

What You Do

1. For each bookmark, cut a piece of construction paper or poster board 6 inches long and 1- to 2-inches wide.

2. Optional: For wavy or jagged edges, cut the paper with pinking shears or other decorative-edge scissors.

3. Decorate the bookmarks with markers, colored pencils, or watercolors. You can also use decorative materials such as stickers, photos, glue, glitter, adhesive-backed craft-foam shapes, or rubber stamps and stamp pads.

4. Write our memory verse (Psalm 81:1) on the back of the bookmark.

5. Cover the bookmark with clear Con-Tact paper for a glossy protective finish. Trim the Con-Tact paper close to the edges of the paper.

6. Punch a hole in the top of the bookmark and tie on a 5-inch piece of ribbon.

God Can Lift You Up

Movie Night

> Be humble in front of the Lord. And he will lift you up.
> James 4:10

Friday after school, Brianna rushed in the door. "Hey, Mom. Hannah invited me to a movie tonight! Can I go?" Brianna threw her backpack in the coat closet.

"Which movie is it?" Mom placed a batch of brownies in the oven.

"Um, I forget the name of it, but all the girls are going." Brianna sat down on a kitchen stool.

"Call Hannah and find out," Mom said. "Then I'll talk with your dad when he gets home."

"All right." Brianna reached for the phone.

On the third ring, Hannah answered the phone. "Hello?"

"Hi, Hannah. It's me, Brianna. What's the name of the movie we're seeing?" Brianna paced the floor in the kitchen. "I forgot and my mom wants to know."

"*Secret Mission,*" Hannah said. "I'll see you at six. Bye."

"So," Mom said. "What did Hannah say?"

"It's called *Secret Mission.*"

171

Your dad and I will talk and then get back to you."

"I'll be in my room waiting." Brianna's voice shook. As she lay on her bed, she thought about one other time her parents didn't let her go somewhere with her friends. She felt left out and thought about sneaking out of the house and going anyway.

"Brianna," Dad said. "Come downstairs, we need to talk with you."

Here goes nothing. "What's the verdict?" Brianna asked the minute her parents sat on the couch downstairs.

"Sorry, Brianna. We researched the movie on a Christian website, and they don't recommend this film for kids your age," Mom said.

Brianna sank in the chair with her arms folded tightly across her chest. She couldn't believe her parents wouldn't let her go to the movies with her friends. "I bet I'm the only one who doesn't get to go!" she said a little louder than she wanted to.

"You know our rules," Dad said. "We don't believe this movie is something we want you to see. We'll try again next time."

Brianna didn't think her friends would invite her next time. This was the second time this happened and probably the last time she'd be invited. Brianna ran out of the room and straight to her bedroom and shut the door. She walked over to her bed, grabbed her pillow and squeezed it tight. She sat down and stared at the wall.

"Brianna," Mom said, "Hannah is on the phone."

"OK." Brianna slowly got up to talk with her friend. "Hey, I can't go." Brianna said.

"Why?" Hannah asked.

"My parents don't think it's for kids our age," Brianna said. "Is there any other movie you'd like to see?"

"No," Hannah said. "All the girls want to see *Secret Mission*. Maybe you and I can go to a different movie some other time."

"OK," Brianna said. "Tell me all about it at school on Monday."

After hanging up the phone, Brianna surprisingly felt pretty good. She still remembered what it felt like to miss out, but she was glad her parents cared enough to find out about the movie. Maybe they do know best. *Thank you, God, for making me feel better*, she prayed silently.

"Hey, Brianna," Dad said. "Why don't we go out for dinner, rent a movie, and eat brownies?"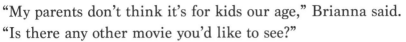

"All right," Brianna said. She still wished she could go out with her friends, but was glad she didn't have to miss out on brownies, her favorite dessert.

MOVIE

Your Turn

1. What kinds of things make you mad at your parents? What do you do when you feel mad?

2. How can you be respectful to your parents when you're mad at them? How can God help you be respectful?

Bible Story

The Parable of the Lost Son

Read Luke 15:11–32

Find the Missing Word

They celebrated with a ___ ___ ___ ___ ◯ !

23

Write About It

In the Parable of the Lost Son, what was the father's response to his son when the son returned home? Why did the brother get jealous?

According to our memory verse, what is God's response when his children are humble?

Tiny Treasure

God will lift you up!

Prayer

Lord God, thank you for lifting me up when I'm down. Help me to humble myself and know your love for me. In Jesus' name, amen.

Do It!

In the Parable of the Lost Son, when the son returned home, he was treated with love and respect instead of treated poorly. In the same way, when you are humbled or humble yourself, you can go to your Heavenly Father and he will lift you up. Try this fun science experiment to illustrate being lifted up.

Air Lift

Object of the Experiment

Lift a book with just air.

What You Need

- Gallon-sized resealable plastic bag

- Heavy book

- Pencil

- Plastic drinking straw

- Packing tape or duct tape

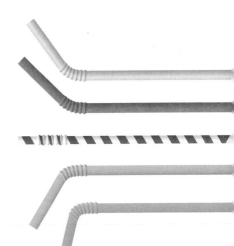

What You Do

1. Place a heavy book on top of the plastic bag. Make sure there is at least two inches of the bag sticking out from under the book on all sides.

2. Poke a hole in the bag with the pencil. Stick the straw in the hole and use tape to seal around the straw so that no air can escape.

3. Blow into the straw. Place your tongue over the straw when taking a breath so that no air can escape. Keep blowing until the book lifts up!

How It Works

When you blow air into the plastic bag, the air is compressed or pushed together. This compressed air pushes on the bag, which makes the book lift up. The plastic bag with the compressed air can support the weight of the book. Can you think of other things you could lift with a plastic bag? Try it!

God's Tender Loving Care

> Turn all your worries over to him. He cares about you.
> 1 Peter 5:7

Can I Have a Pet?

One Saturday, Savannah cradled Rachel's white bunny. Savannah asked Rachel, "How did you get your parents to buy Whiskers for you?"

"Well," Rachel said, "I promised to feed him, clean his cage, and make sure he has fresh water. If I don't, my parents deduct money from my allowance. So far, I haven't lost any money."

Savannah put Whiskers in his cage and gave him a carrot to nibble. "When my mom picks me up, maybe she can see Whiskers. "I can tell her how I've been caring for him today. Maybe she'll let me get an animal of my own."

Rachel said, "I hope so." The girls heard Rachel's mom call from the house. "I'll be right back," Rachel went in the house.

Having a moment to herself, Savannah decided to pray to God.

Dear Father God, you know how much I want a pet. Please give me the courage to talk to my parents again about having a pet—maybe a rabbit like Rachel's. I've tried to be more responsible lately. My grades are OK, and I've been trying to do my chores before being asked. Having a pet isn't a serious thing, but the Bible says to bring

my worries to you because you care for me. Please . . . Help me be brave enough to ask again. Thank you for hearing my prayers. In Jesus' name, amen.

Later, when Savannah's mom arrived to take her home, Savannah asked. "Mom, can I show you something?"

"Sure," Mom said.

Savannah's stomach clenched as they made their way to the rabbit's cage. She pointed to the bunny.

"Oh," Mom said. "How cute."

"Do you want to hold him?" Rachel asked.

Savannah's eyes lit up. "I do!" She stretched out her arms to hold the bunny.

"Savannah helped me take care of Whiskers today," Rachel said. "She's very good with animals."

"Rachel taught me a lot about the responsibility of having a pet. I think I'm ready." Savannah bravely continued. "Can we go to the pet store on the way home?"

"We can go look today," Mom said. "I'll need to discuss it with your dad before we buy an animal, but I think you may be ready."

"All right!" Savannah smiled as she handed Whiskers back to Rachel. *God helped me*, she thought. *God does care about me!*

Your Turn

1. Do you have a pet that you care for? What kind of animal is it? What things do you to do care for it?

2. What are some ways God shows that he cares for you?

Bible Story

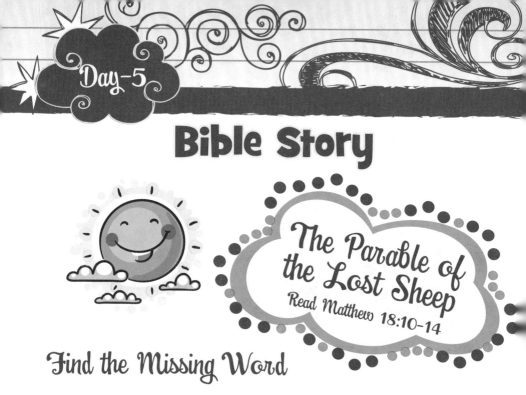

The Parable of the Lost Sheep
Read Matthew 18:10-14

Find the Missing Word

The shepherd looks for the ___ ___ ___ that has wandered off.

Write About It

In the Parable of the Lost Sheep, why did the man go look for the one lost sheep when he had ninety-nine others?

Tell about a time when God took care of you.

Tiny Treasure

God cares about everything about you!

Prayer

Lord God, thank you for caring for me. Help me to learn how to care for others. In Jesus' name, amen.

Do It!

Just as the shepherd went out to look for the lost sheep, God makes sure that his children are always taken care of. You can show the same loving care for an animal whether it is a family pet or even pets without homes. Try making these doggy treats to give to your dog if you have one, a friend's dot, or a local animal shelter.

Yummy Dog Biscuits

What You Need

- Measuring cup
- 1¼ cups grated cheddar cheese
- ¼ pound corn oil margarine, softened
- 1½ cups whole-wheat flour, plus additional for flouring cutting board
- 1 crushed garlic clove
- Mixing bowl
- Mixing spoon
- Milk
- Plastic wrap
- Cutting board
- Rolling pin
- Butter knife or bone-shaped cookie cutter

What You Do

1. Combine all the ingredients and mix well.

2. Add enough milk to form the dough into a big ball. Cover the ball with plastic wrap and chill in the refrigerator for 30 minutes.

3. Sprinkle flour on a cutting board. Roll out the dough to about a ½-inch thickness. Cut out bone shapes.

4. On an ungreased cookie sheet, bake at 375°F for 15 minutes or slightly brown and firm.

5. Makes 24–36 biscuits.

God Forgives

God is faithful and fair. If we confess our sins, he will forgive our sins. He will forgive every wrong thing we have done. He will make us pure.

1 John 1:9

Jessica stared at the books, toys, and paper that were scattered around her room. "MOM! Tyler must have been playing in my room again!" Jessica looked at her favorite book angrily. Pages were torn and there were scribble marks on every page.

"Oh, no. I'm so sorry, Jessica." Mom shook her head. The telephone started ringing. Mom said, "I'll be right back."

Angry thoughts swirled through Jessica's head as she started picking up her room. *Why did my parents have to adopt a toddler? He's such a pain!*

After her room was clean, Jessica sat on her bed, paging through her ruined book.

Mom walked in and joined Jessica on her bed.

"Mom, why does Tyler want to wreck my things?" Tears formed in Jessica's eyes.

Mom rubbed Jessica's arm. "Your brother is only two years old. I will have him apologize to you," Mom said.

"Tell him never to do it again!" Jessica folded her arms across her chest.

"You need to forgive him, Jessica." Mom took hold of her right hand. "Do you remember when you spilled my favorite perfume all over the bathroom floor?"

Jessica felt her face heat up. "Yes."

"I think you were even older than Tyler," Mom said, making her point. "I forgave you and didn't love you any less because of it. God wants his children to confess their sins to him. When they do he will forgive. God wants us to forgive others the same way he forgives us." There was a cry from the other room. "Tyler's awake," Mom said. "I'll be right back."

Jessica had a lot to think about. *Mom DID forgive her about the perfume right away—*

"Tyler would like to tell you something." Mom held Tyler in her arms.

"Sorry." Tyler hid his face in his hands.

Jessica opened up his hands as if they were playing peek-a-boo. "I forgive you."

"We'll go buy you a new book tomorrow," Mom said.

"That's OK," Jessica said. "I can look for it at the library."

"That's my girl." Mom hugged both Jessica and Tyler tight.

Your Turn

1. When are some times it might be hard to forgive someone else? When have you had a hard time forgiving someone? Is there someone you need to forgive now?

2. What does our verse mean when it says God is faithful and fair? How does it make you feel to know that God will always be faithful and fair to you?

Bible Story

Find the Missing Word

Whatever you bind, or lock, on ___ ___ ___ ___ ◯

2

will be bound in heaven.

Write About It

What was the response of the father when his son came home?
What was his brother's response?

Describe a time when it was difficult to forgive someone, but you did it anyway.

Tiny Treasure

God forgives!

Prayer

Lord God, thank you for being faithful and just, and for forgiving my sins. In Jesus' name, amen.

Do It!

Just as the father forgave his son in the story of the prodigal son, you too, can forgive others. Forgiving others brings us closer to our Heavenly Father. Try this fun activity to understand forgiveness.

Closer to God by Forgiving

This object lesson demonstrates the power of God's forgiveness over our sins, and how the Holy Spirit can melt away the barriers that keep us from him.

What You Need

- Small glass or cup

- 3 nickels

- Two-ply bathroom tissue

- Rubber band

- Eyedropper

- Water

What You Do

1. Separate the two-ply bathroom tissue into two thin squares. (Some two-ply facial tissue also works well.)

2. Take one separated tissue square and place it over the opening of the glass. Secure square with the rubber band, forming something like a drum.

3. Place three nickels on the tissue near the center. Pick up some water in the eyedropper and place a few drops of water on the tissue just around and next to the nickels.

What Will Happen

After about 30–60 seconds, the tissue will break and the nickels will fall into the cup.

What It Means

For this example, God is like the cup and we are like the nickels. God wants us to be his children and live close to him. However, sin and fear (the tissue) can keep us from being with him. God wants us (the nickels) to trust him, so the Holy Spirit (water) helps us to know and trust God. When we listen to the Holy Spirit and ask for forgiveness in our hearts, God will forgive us (melting away of the tissue) and we can live forever with him (being in the cup).

God's Mercy

So have mercy, just as your Father has mercy.
Luke 6:36

The Birthday Card

A knock sounded at Lauren's door. "Hey, sweetie," Mom said. "Are you ready for some cake and ice cream?"

"In a minute, Mom," Lauren said, wiping her eyes. Every year on her birthday, her dad was away on business. She wondered why her dad accepted the job, knowing how much he would be away from home. Anger and resentment built in Lauren's heart. She opened her door and was surprised to see her grandmother. "Hi, Grandma!" *Why can't my dad come home, too?*

"Come on everyone," Mom said. "The ice cream's melting!"

Once seated, her mom lit the candles and they sang the birthday song. Lauren made a secret wish and blew out the candles.

Mom reached into a drawer and pulled out an envelope. "This is for you."

Lauren ripped open the envelope to find a card from her dad.

> Dear Lauren,
>
> I love you so much. I hope you have a very special day. When I get home, we'll celebrate! Sorry I can't be with you on your birthday.
>
> Much love,
> Dad

193

Lauren stared at the words her dad wrote. Did he really love her? If he did, then why wasn't he home instead of on a business trip? Lauren looked up at her mom and Grandma. "I can't wait to try some of that chocolate cake," Lauren said, hoping no one would ask her questions about the card from her dad.

"So, Lauren," said Grandma, "Did you get a nice card from your dad?"

"Uh, yeah." Lauren dug into her cake taking a huge bite.

"What did he say?" probed her grandma.

Lauren answered. "He wants me to have a special day. With you here, Grandma, it sure is!"

"Is that all it says?" Grandma took a sip of coffee.

"And . . . that he loves me."

"That's wonderful!" Mom said.

Lauren remembered all the cards her dad had written to her over the years. He never forgot her birthday and always wrote something special. "You know, I think I'm starting to understand."

"Understand what, honey?" asked Grandma.

"Dad loves me and is working hard for our family!" Lauren said. "I've been kind of mad at him, but now I think I've forgiven him for not being here."

Mom nodded. "I'm proud of you!"

"Yeah." Lauren smiled. "Can we open some gifts now?"

Laughter erupted all around the table.

Your Turn

1. Do you sometimes have a difficult time forgiving others? Why? What could help you be more forgiving?

2. Having mercy is kind of like forgiveness. It means letting someone off the hook and showing them forgiveness or kindness, even though you don't have to. How do you know that God is merciful?

Bible Story

The Parable of the Unmerciful Servant
Read Matthew 18: 21-35

Find the Missing Word

The servant's master canceled the ⭘ ___ ___ ___ and let him go

22

Write About It

In his parable of the unmerciful servant, Jesus says we must forgive someone how many times?

Tell of a time when you showed mercy to someone even though it was tough.

Tiny Treasure

when you need it, God will show mercy to you!

Prayer

Lord God, thank you for being merciful. Help me to forgive others. In Jesus' name, amen.

Do It!

Just as the King cancelled the servant's debt in the Parable of the Merciful Servant, God shows mercy to his children. You too, can show mercy to others.

Learn more about mercy below, and then make ABC soup with a parent to remind you of the message of mercy.

The message of mercy is that God loves us—all of us—no matter how great our sins. He wants us to recognize that his mercy is greater than our sins, so that we will call upon him with trust, receive his mercy, and let it flow through us to others. One simple way to remember this is with our ABCs:

A. Ask for his Mercy. God wants us to approach him in prayer constantly, repenting of our sins and asking him to pour his mercy out upon us and upon the whole world.

B. Be merciful. God wants us to receive his mercy and let it flow through us to others. He wants us to extend love and forgiveness to others just as he does to us.

C. Completely trust in Jesus. God wants us to know that the graces of his mercy are dependent upon our trust. The more we trust in Jesus, the more we will receive.

ABC Soup

What You Need

- 1 medium onion, diced (1 cup)

- 2 teaspoon vegetable oil

- 1½ cups carrots peeled and diced

- 1 48-ounce can chicken stock

- 1 cup diced celery

- 1 cup miniature alphabet pasta or 1½ cups medium egg noodles

What You Do

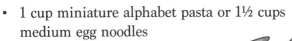

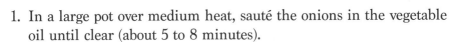

1. In a large pot over medium heat, sauté the onions in the vegetable oil until clear (about 5 to 8 minutes).

2. Add the carrots and chicken stock, cover the pot, and bring to a boil. Reduce the heat and simmer for 10 minutes.

3. Add the celery and simmer another 5 minutes, stirring occasionally.

4. Turn off the heat and stir in the pasta.* Cover the pot and let sit for 20 minutes (15 minutes if you're using egg noodles).

Enjoy! Or, let it cool and store it in the refrigerator. Makes 7 cups.

* Keep in mind that the secret to perfectly cooked noodles is not to cook them. Just let them soften in the warm broth.

God Sends You

> God began a good work in you.
> And I am sure that he will carry it
> on until it is completed. That will be on
> the day Christ Jesus returns.
>
> Philippians 1:6

Music to My Ears

Well, here goes nothing, Emily thought as she entered the nursing home with her stepmom, Sandy. Double doors were opened wide to a room full of older people. Some were sitting in wheelchairs while others sat on couches around the room. Emily noticed smiles on some of their faces. She rubbed her hands down the sides of her jean skirt, hoping to dry them off before playing the piano. This was more nerve wracking than the piano recital!

"Hello, everyone," Sandy said. "We have a special treat for you today. My stepdaughter, Emily, is here to play the piano for you."

Emily sat down at the piano, and noticed a lady seated nearby. The lady wore her hair in a bun with small ringlets surrounding her wrinkled face. Her dress was made of velvet and lace. She wore white gloves on her neatly folded hands. Emily started playing her song. She pretended she was in a famous concert hall and the little old lady was a queen, nodding her head in approval.

When Emily played the last note of the song, Sandy announced, "Refreshments will now be served."

Emily stood up from the piano bench and walked the short distance to the fancy old lady and said, "Hello."

"Why, hello, dear," the old lady said. "Would you like to have cookies with me?" She patted the space next to her on the floral couch.

"Sure," Emily said.

Once seated, a nursing home employee came up to them with a plate full of cookies. "Miss Donovan, I have your favorite chocolate mint cookies."

"Why, thank you, Rose," Miss Donovan said. Rose handed her a napkin and two cookies. "Rose always brings me my favorite cookies. She knows I can't pick them out for myself, because I'm blind!"

Emily remembered Sandy talking about a wonderful blind lady that lived at the nursing home. Could this be the same lady? Emily looked carefully into Miss Donovan's eyes. She couldn't imagine what it would be like to be blind. "Do you like piano music?" Emily asked, not knowing what else to say.

"Oh, yes, dear. Will you play some more? My ears work just fine." Miss Donovan leaned toward Emily and smiled.

At that moment, Sandy stood in the front of the room and looked right at Emily. "Emily, would you please play another song for us?"

As Emily stood up and headed to the piano, she understood why Sandy came every week to the nursing home to spend time with the older people. She hoped Sandy would ask her to come back again.

Your Turn

1. What are some ways kids your age can do a good work and help others? Helping others is a way we can show that we follow Jesus. What are some of your favorite ways to help others?

2. Our verse says that God began a good work in you. What good work do you think God has in mind for you? What are some of the gifts he has given you?

Bible Story

The Great Commission
Read Matthew 28:16-20

Find the Missing Word

The disciples went to the ___ ◯ ___ ___ ___ ___ ___

13

where Jesus told them.

Write About It

What did Jesus tell the disciples to do in today's Bible reading?

This applies to Jesus' followers today the same as it did to the disciples. What does Jesus want us to do? What are some of the things you can do to share Jesus with others?

Tiny Treasure

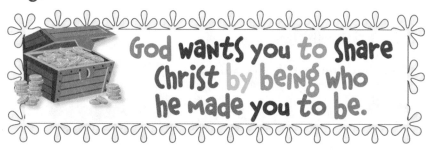

God **wants** you to **share** Christ by being who he made you to be.

Prayer

Lord God, thank you for creating me. Help me to continue to grow into the person you want me to be. In Jesus' name, amen.

Do It!

Just as the father forgave his son in the story of the prodigal son, you too, can forgive others. Forgiving others brings us closer to our Heavenly Father. Try this fun activity to understand forgiveness.

Pen Pals for Jesus

Wouldn't it be fun to write to someone and have them write back? There are several ways you can do this activity.

1. You can ask your pastor or Sunday school teacher to find another church, somewhere in either the United States or abroad, for your class to partner with and exchange letters or emails.

2. You can search the Internet with a parent to find someone with your specific area of interest (music, sports, art, drama, writing, etc.) to correspond with.

3. Your family can sponsor a child through World Vision International. With your parent's help, you can research online to see what is involved in helping a child across the globe. You can exchange letters with your sponsored child with an interpreter to translate if needed.

God's Unchanging Ways

Jesus Christ is the same yesterday and today and forever.
Hebrews 13:8

Life Changes

Brianna sat in the back row of the bus. Two more stops until she could get off. Even with the windows down as far as they would go, she felt like a fried egg on a hot skillet. It felt more like summer outside than the beginning of spring.

Hannah sat next to her on the bus. "Brianna, do we have a spelling test this Friday?"

"Yeah," Brianna said, discouraged at the thought. Spelling was by far her worst subject. "Gotta go. Here's my stop."

She kicked the dirt under her feet as she walked the long block home. What was worse than spelling was the fact that her parents told her that they'd be moving to another state once their house sold.

"Hi, Brianna," Mom said once she entered the house.

"I'm going to my room." Brianna headed up the stairs.

Brianna sat on her bed and stared out the window. These days, her feelings were all over the place. One minute she was happy, the next sad. Why did her moods change? Her mom said it was because it was hard to think about leaving her school, church, and all her friends.

She really liked her house and didn't want to move.

She grabbed her math book from her backpack, sat at her desk, and started her homework.

"Brianna," Mom called, "Hannah's on the phone for you."

"Coming!"

"Can you give me the spelling words for the test this Friday? I forgot mine at school."

After spelling all of the words, Brianna hung up the phone. She was about to go back upstairs, but her mom stopped her and gave her a hug. She didn't say anything. Just hugged her and watched her go back to her room.

Brianna sat on her bed still thinking about the hug her mom gave her. She remembered how scared she was the last time the family moved. It worked out, even though it took a while to get used to everything. Brianna reached over and pulled open the drawer to her end table. She pulled the bookmark her mom made for her out of her Bible. Hebrews 13:8 was written on it. It said, "Jesus is the same yesterday and today and forever."

Brianna smiled, glad to know that no matter how life changed, God would be there for her no matter what.

Your Turn

1. When do you feel your moods changing? Is there something in particular that can make you go from glad to mad? Is there something going on in your life that is changing soon?

2. How does it make you feel to know that God is unchanging?

Bible Story

The Certainty of God's Promise
Read Hebrews 6:13-20

Find the Missing Word

The hope we have is an ___ ___ ___ ◯ ___ ___

8

for the soul, firm, and secure.

Write About It

In today's Bible reading, what did God want the people to whom he'd made a promise to know? (Write verse 17.)

How has God shown his promises to you? From the promises from God that you've read about in this book, which is your favorite? If you haven't done so already, memorize this promise.

Tiny Treasure

God will always be there for you!

Prayer

Lord God, thank you that you are the same yesterday and today and forever. In Jesus' name, amen.

Do It!

Just as God is unchanging so are his promises. You too, can greatly be encouraged by God's promises just like Abram and others from the Bible. Try this crossword puzzle to learn about some of God's promises.

Look up the references in your Bible to find the answers.

God's Promises Crossword

Across

4. God promised to make this great (Genesis 12:2).

5. God will write his law on this (Jeremiah 31:33).

6. God promised to give this to Abram's descendants (Genesis 12:7).

8. God promised to make him into a great nation (Genesis 12:1-2).

9. The people here would be blessed through Abram (Genesis 12:3).

10 God made a new one with the house of Israel and Judah (Jeremiah 31:31).

11. God will remember this no more (Jeremiah 31:34).

Down

1. Promise of this to the Israelites if they obeyed God (Deuteronomy 28:2).

2. Promise of this to the Israelites if they disobeyed God (Deuteronomy 28:15).

3. God promised that this would be established forever (2 Samuel 7:16).

4. God promised to save this person along with his family from the flood (Genesis 6:9,18).

7. Was a sign never to destroy the earth again by a flood (Genesis 9:11–13).

*Answers found on page 220.

God Wins

Let us give thanks to God! He gives us the victory because of what our Lord Jesus Christ has done.
1 Corinthians 15:57

V for Victory

"I win," Savannah said to her dad as she finished him off in a game of checkers. "How about another round? Best two out of three?"

"OK, since you are such a good sport." Dad put the checkers back in place.

"I smell the scent of victory already." Savannah rubbed her hands together.

"Hold on there, Squirt. Where is that good sport I was talking about?"

"Sorry, Dad," Savannah said. "Ready?"

The game started at a fast pace with both Savannah and her dad making quick moves with their checkers. Then Savannah had the next turn. She took a sip of her water bottle to stall for time.

"Your move," Dad said.

Savannah concentrated. She spotted a move where she could jump three of her dad's checkers. "Your turn."

"Ah, I see what you're doing," Dad gave Savannah a sly grin.

"You won't get these three checkers yet." He moved a checker out of the line of fire.

"I will soon." Savannah grinned. She looked carefully at her red checkers wanting to keep all the back checkers in place until she absolutely needed them. "I think I will have to sacrifice one." She moved a red checker next to one of her dad's black ones.

"Thanks for the tip." Her dad jumped the red checker.

For the next ten minutes, Savannah and her dad took turns jumping each

213

 other's checkers hoping to be the last one standing. It came down to three red to two black. Savannah cornered one of her dad's black checkers. "That one's toast."

"You're right." Dad nodded. "Good thing I have this king over here."

After jumping the cornered black checker, Savannah noticed that one of her red checkers was also cornered. She didn't say anything to her dad in case he didn't see it.

Dad jumped two red checkers. "Sorry, Squirt."

Savannah frowned. "I didn't see that double jump."

"We each have one left," Dad said. "We could be playing all night!"

"Unless you let me win!" Savannah gave her dad a sweet smile and batted her eyelashes.

"Would you really want me to do that?" Dad asked.

"Sure," Savannah said. "Like you said, Dad, this could go on all night."

"Wouldn't you like to win fair and square?" Dad asked.

"I guess you're right."

They continued to take turns. Savannah yawned.

"It's getting late," Dad said. "Want to pick up where we left off in the morning?"

"I'll dream of checkers all night unless we finish." Savannah absentmindedly placed her red checker where she could be jumped.

"Game's over, Squirt." Dad jumped the final red checker. "I win."

"What just happened?" Savannah folded her arms.

"We each won a game," Dad said. "I think it's time for you to go to bed."

"I should have paid more attention." Savannah packed up the game.

"It's hard to lose," Dad said. "But that's life sometimes. Sometimes you lose, and sometimes you win."

"That reminds me of something," Savannah said. "Last Sunday my Sunday school teacher taught us a verse that says we can all have victory through Jesus! What do you think, Dad? You and Mom want to join me tomorrow morning at church?"

"OK, Squirt, you win!" Dad said. "We'll come."

She hugged her dad around the neck. "I need to call Jessica and tell her I don't need a ride!"

Your Turn

1. What are some of the games you like to play? Are you a good sport or a bad sport if you lose? Why?

2. What does it mean to you when our verse says that God gives us victory because of Jesus Christ?

215

Bible Story

Faith in the Son of God

Read 1 John 5:1-12

Find the Missing Word

Everyone born of God overcomes the —— —— —— —— ◯ .

7

Write About It

Write I John 5:4–5 in your own words. What does this mean to you?

When and how will you celebrate your victory in Christ Jesus?

Tiny Treasure

God Shows us how to WIN!

Prayer

Lord God, thank you that I have the victory because of your Son, Jesus Christ! In Jesus' name I pray, amen.

Do It!

The Bible tells us we have victory in Christ. This means you can be assured of your place in heaven. Try making this fun decorative pillow to remind you of your victory in Jesus!

Victory Pillow

What You Need

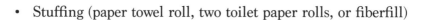

- 1 pair of old jeans

- 2 rubber bands

- 2 ties (leather, yarn, ribbons, string)

- Stuffing (paper towel roll, two toilet paper rolls, or fiberfill)

- Decorations (beads, fabric paint, button, etc.)

What You Do

- Cut one leg off a pair of old jeans. Wash the pant leg a few times to get a frayed look and then dry in the dryer.

- Fill the pant leg with a paper towel roll, two toilet paper rolls, or stuffing depending on what you like or what fits the best.

- Tie both ends of the jean leg with rubber bands making sure that it is even on both sides.

- Tie ribbons, leather, yarn or string to both ends of the jean pillow on top of the rubber bands.

- Decorate your pillow!

Alternate Ideas

- To make it officially a victory pillow, make a big V using fabric paint in the center of the pillow. Or you can write "Victory in Jesus!"

- You can hot glue (with parent help) some fun buttons or beads on your pillow, too!

Appendices

IN GOD WE TRUST MONEY GAME ANSWER KEY

1. **9**	5. **9**
2. **3**	6. **4**
3. **10**	7. **8**
4. **7**	

GOD'S PROMISES CROSSWORD ANSWER KEY

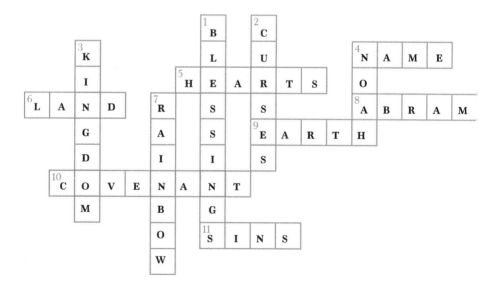

FIND THE MISSING WORDS ANSWER KEY

Page 12: Child

Page 18: Heart

Page 24: Forty

Page 30: Love

Page 36: Feet

Page 44: Lamp

Page 51: Eye

Page 58: Kingdom

Page 64: Door

Page 71: House

Page 78: Boat

Page 84: Rest

Page 91: Eighteen

Page 97: Good soil

Page 104: Heaven

Page 111: Twelve

Page 118: Ghost

Page 124: Manna

Page 132: Tree

Page 139: Branches

Page 146: Cross

Page 153: Towel

Page 160: Rooms

Page 167: Silver

Page 175: Feast

Page 182: One

Page 189: Earth

Page 196: Debt

Page 203: Mountain

Page 209: Anchor

Page 216: World

Secret Message
The Lord has promised good things!

A Note for Teachers and Parents

SOME IDEAS FOR HOW TO USE THIS BOOK:

1. Read the Bible verses one after the other for an uplifting time of worship.

2. Allow tween girls to have their own private thoughts with the "Your Turn" and "Write about It" sections.

3. Study the whole book together, sharing with each other thoughts and feelings. Yes, you need to share too!

4. Give this book to a child as her own private journal, making sure to join her in the "Do It" sections when appropriate.

These promises of God keep us going on a daily basis. Why not share them as a class or family?

Blessings,

Sherry Kyle

Be sure to look for more True Heart Girls devotionals by Sherry Kyle.

Find these and more great books for kids at
www.HendricksonRose.com.